THE DEADLY

DISEASES THEN AND NOW

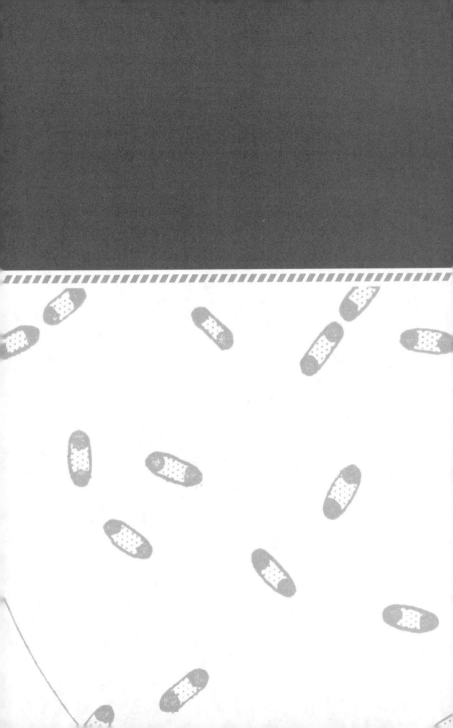

THE DEADLIEST

DISEASES THEN AND NOW

BY

**DEBORAH
HOPKINSON**

SCHOLASTIC
FOCUS
NEW YORK

Library of Congress Cataloging-in-Publication Data available

ISBN   978-1-338-36022-6

1 2021

Printed in the U.S.A.   23
First edition, October 2021

Book design by Abby Dening

Illustration, previous page: A book illustration showing highly magnified plague bacilli. Note the rod shape.

*In memory of those lost to COVID-19
and with gratitude to health care workers, scientists, and
all those on the front lines of the coronavirus pandemic*

Contents

A dead plague-infected rat. After their rat hosts die, rat fleas infected with plague bacteria may spread plague to other warm-blooded creatures, including people.

PROLOGUE

Then: The Fourteenth Century

Imagine you're living in Genoa, Italy, a long time ago—let's say the fall of 1347. It's the **medieval era**, or **Middle Ages**, a long period in history from the years 500 to 1500.

Naturally, you've never seen a car, bus, train, or plane. Put things like cell phones, television, electricity, and computers out of your mind. Why, you're lucky you know how to read and write—most ordinary people at this time didn't get the chance to learn. Many were peasants, who had little of their own and worked in the fields for nobles or rich landowners.

But you're lucky that way too. Your family is doing well. Your father's a Genoese merchant who does business around much of the world. In the fall of 1347 he's away, overseeing an expedition to the Black Sea region.

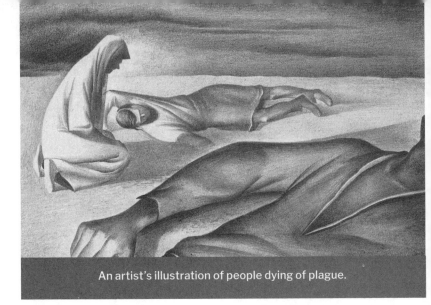
An artist's illustration of people dying of plague.

He's shown it to you on a map. You know his ship will sail down the coast of Italy, then head east across the Mediterranean Sea and into the Aegean Sea. From there, he'll pass the gateway city of Constantinople and thread his way through the Turkish Straits. He'll cross the Black Sea to reach the wonderful harbor of Caffa, a far-off trading post owned by Genoa.

Your father will return with silver, spices, rye, wheat, and other grains to sell. He's promised to bring your mother luxurious silk fabric from China. And when autumn comes, you stand on the hillside overlooking Genoa's harbor and keep watch for him.

The ships finally arrive, but your father does not. Something terrible has happened. You listen at the door when men bring your mother the news. A few strange, scary words reach your ears: *painful boils, fever, sickness, death.*

You're still in shock when horrible things start to happen in your own city. Life changes overnight: A dreadful disease races through Genoa like wildfire. The bustling market square nearby is eerily quiet and deserted. The shops and piazzas are empty. You watch neighbors loading up carts with their worldly goods. They're fleeing to the countryside, hoping to outrun this invisible, terrifying thing.

It is a great pestilence, a deadly disease. It is **plague**.

The onslaught doesn't stop. Entire families disappear behind the walls of their houses, never to be seen again. Your mother refuses to let you leave home. You know she's worried your food will soon run out. Your little brother cries in hunger.

One day, you spy a dead body being removed from the house next door, wrapped in a sheet, ready to be taken to the parish church. You open the door a crack. Is that your friend? But you slam the door shut quickly. The stench is sickening.

There are no solemn funeral processions anymore. No religious services or gatherings of friends and family. Before long, you get used to seeing corpses carried through the streets on plain boards. Sometimes you watch priests or doctors enter nearby homes. They always come out hanging their heads, worn down by sorrow. Despite the comfort they offer and the treatments they use, many patients are dying.

In your home, only one loyal servant remains. She says she's heard what this awful affliction does to people. At first, victims feel light-headed and sick to their stomach. They complain of headache, chills, and fever. Soon painful, smelly lumps, called **buboes**, erupt on their body, either on the neck or in the armpit or groin.

She tells you stories of other victims, who cough and spit up a bloody mucus. They can't catch their breath. Anyone who comes near them falls ill too. Entire households perish within days. A few people with buboes get better. No one who has a bloody cough ever does.

Your mother burns incense and fragrant herbs to purify the air. She wrings her hands and prays. She says this great pestilence is punishment from an angry God.

Nothing in your life is the same. You spend your days shaking in fear, worried your family will be next. You don't want to die.

In your heart, you know the end of the world has come.

It's not easy, from a distance of nearly seven hundred years, to imagine what life was like during the **Great Mortality**, or "great death," the plague **outbreak** that struck western Europe, Central Asia, the Middle East, and many parts of Africa in the mid-1300s. While some people refer to this outbreak as the **Black Death**, here we'll call it by the name used by those who lived through it.

Deadly pandemics like the Great Mortality have mostly seemed quite distant from modern life in the twenty-first century. Even the terror of a horrific **influenza pandemic** in 1918, just over a hundred years ago, has been largely forgotten in our time.

These terrible events seemed like things just to read about in history books. It seemed impossible—unthinkable—that people's lives would be turned upside down like that ever again.

Then, in late 2019, a new, unknown **coronavirus** (**SARS-CoV-2**) emerged in China, jumping from animals to infect humans. The **virus** causes a disease named **COVID-19**, which can be mild or very serious. In early 2020, the world changed quickly, much as it had done in Italy—as well as everywhere else in Europe, the Middle East, and North Africa— so long ago.

Businesses and schools shut down. Families sheltered in place. Some fled the cities, hoping to be safer in the countryside. People changed their behavior to try to slow the spread of the disease.

We began wearing face masks. We didn't hug friends. We listened to **epidemiologists**, scientists who study the patterns of disease. We learned new terms such as **physical distancing**, which means not getting too close to others, since that lessens the chance virus particles in the air will infect others when they are breathed out.

And something else happened too. People of all ages became more curious about pandemics of the past. We remembered that human beings have faced deadly diseases many times before.

This book is about some of those diseases. We'll explore plague, the 1918 influenza pandemic, and a few other diseases, from the past and now.

We'll begin with the Great Mortality. Though we can't really go back in time and truly understand what it was like to live through it, we can try.

And perhaps our own experiences *now* will help us better imagine *then*.

A stowaway rat on a cart. Rats infected with plague bacteria can pass the disease to fleas that may then bite and infect humans.

Part One

THE GREAT MORTALITY

"And were it not for the fact that I am one of many people who saw it with their own eyes, I would scarcely dare to believe it, let alone commit it to paper . . ."

— GIOVANNI BOCCACCIO, ITALY

CHAPTER 1
Calling All Disease Detectives

P lague. The very word has the power to make us afraid. No wonder—there's no other disease like it. Powerful and deadly, plague has been around for thousands of years. And because the plague **bacterium** circulates naturally in various animal populations, we can't ever get rid of it. Plague will always be with us.

Plague has sometimes crossed over into humans, causing death, devastation, and major changes to society. It's a complex disease, with different forms, symptoms, ways of spreading, and outcomes. It took humans centuries to understand how it works. It ranks with smallpox as one of the deadliest diseases in history.

Nothing about the story of plague is simple.

Investigating the Great Mortality

Historians estimate that plague has killed more than 200 million people, though there is no way to know for sure. There have been three massive outbreaks, or pandemics, of plague in recorded history. There could have been other outbreaks in the past that we just don't know much about yet. The Great Mortality, which erupted in the mid-1300s during plague's Second Pandemic, was the most ferocious.

The Great Mortality took place from about 1346 to 1353. It caused enormous upheavals in societies across much of the world. In this book we focus primarily on western Europe, where plague reached Italy in late 1347. However, it's important to note that the Great Mortality affected people all across the world, from Central Asia to the Middle East, North Africa, and perhaps Sub-Saharan Africa (the portion of Africa south of the Sahara Desert) as well. In fact, historians now believe that only the Americas, Australia, and Oceania, a region that includes Micronesia and Polynesia, were spared. Some historians put the Great Mortality death toll as high as 40, 50, or even 60 percent of the population across Eurasia (Europe and Asia together) and Africa. That means that five or six out of every ten people died.

Historians are still uncovering evidence to help us understand more about the Great Mortality and its impact on societies throughout the world. And while many books have been written about how the disaster affected Europe, some questions remain here too. When, where, and why did the Great Mortality begin? How did plague get to Italy in the fall of 1347? What was it like on a plague ship? How did plague spread? And was the Great Mortality caused only by plague, or did people die of other diseases too?

To find answers to these and other questions, historians and scientists use **primary sources**, original artifacts, art, or documents like letters and official records. They apply new scientific techniques to analyze physical evidence such as teeth from medieval graveyards. They study archaeological remains, to see how the things left behind by people changed over time. Epidemiologists also use computer models to create a more complete picture of how plague spread.

Many of these tools are being used to help expand our understanding of medieval plague in areas outside Europe. Scholars are conducting new research on how plague spread in places such as Anatolia, which makes up modern-day Turkey, and in Africa, including sub-Saharan Africa. The twenty-first century is an exciting time to look back at the fourteenth century!

These amazing researchers are disease detectives. Their work helps us understand what happened in the past—and enables us to prepare for and manage future pandemics.

For us to learn about the Great Mortality, we need to be detectives too. So put on your thinking cap and let's begin.

Tracing the Path of Plague

We started with an imaginary family in Genoa in the fall of 1347, a time of confusion and fear. If you were living then, you'd never know the truth about the disease that threatened your world. But from where we sit, we can piece together the story.

To begin, let's consider what we know about how diseases spread in our own time. Today, someone with an **infectious disease** (one that can be passed from one person to another like a cold or the flu) can get on a plane and fly across an ocean in just a matter of hours. We ride subways and buses to school or work, hop into cars to visit relatives in other cities, and travel long distances by train. And wherever we go, diseases go with us.

What about the 1300s?

Well, it took a lot longer to get around during the medieval era, but the world was more connected than you might imagine. Invading armies marched across vast distances to conquer new territories. People traded and traveled across the seas by ship. Farmers took produce to villages and towns by carts. Caravans of merchants traveled long distances overland, crossing from place to place, country to country. Closer to home, people visited with family and friends, went shopping, and had many interactions with others in their community.

And just like today, wherever people went, diseases went too.

Of course, piecing together the story of plague isn't like tracking diseases today. In some countries during the 2020 coronavirus pandemic, cell phone applications let users know if they were on the same bus or subway with someone who tested positive for COVID-19. That kind of precise GPS (Global Positioning System) tracking simply didn't exist in the past.

That's why disease detectives have to be a bit like naturalists tracking an animal in the wilderness. We have to look closely for small, subtle clues: a paw print here, a broken branch there, a bit of fur clinging to a twig.

One place to look for clues about plague is in history's written record. Although the printing press wasn't invented until 1440, people wrote on paper, linen, and parchment (treated animal skin). Monks in monasteries copied texts and recorded histories. Sometimes merchants, churches, and cities kept records. Doctors had medical books and records and, much like today, students took notes or made copies of lectures given by teachers and scholars. Rulers liked to have a written account of their achievements and successes in battle.

In addition to these sorts of documents, a few individuals took it upon themselves to record events in a **chronicle**, a written history or record. These **chroniclers** were the journalists, on-the-spot reporters, and history keepers of their time.

They're our guides to the Great Mortality.

The First Clues

To find out how plague burst into Italy in the fall of 1347, we have to start looking far from Europe. We know plague has always been present in some parts of Central and Eastern Asia, where it still circulates in populations of burrowing rodents called marmots, and sometimes crosses into humans. (We'll talk more about marmots and the science behind how plague spreads a bit later.)

Scholars continue to discover more about the possible origins of the Great Mortality. While people used to think the Great Mortality began in the 1330s, recent research points to earlier outbreaks. In fact, we find our first clue in the mid-1200s, a hundred years before the Great Mortality began. Terrible sicknesses were reported at several fortresses and cities that **Mongol** armies had besieged in what is now Iran and Iraq. These sicknesses were most likely plague.

Many decades later, a chronicle reports that in 1332, a Mongol ruler, only twenty-eight years old, and his sons were all felled by a strange illness. Historians think it's likely they all died of plague as well.

Sometimes disease detectives are lucky enough to find physical evidence. That brings us to our next sighting: Gravestones unearthed from 1338–1339 in central Asia, near Lake Issyk Kul (in what is now Kyrgyzstan) reveal that plague was here then.

How do we know? Well, during these two years, there were more gravestones than usual. Something occurred to cause more people to die. One marker reads: "'This is the grave of Kutluk—he died of plague with his wife Magu-kelka.'"

Scholars once assumed that plague outbreaks moved east to west on the Silk Road, an ancient network of trade routes connecting the East and West. In fact, many older books I consulted for this book say just that. However, knowledge about the history of the Great Mortality is constantly changing and being updated as new evidence emerges.

How do we know? Well, I asked medical historian Dr. Lori Jones to read a draft of this book. (She corrected a lot!) She also shared cutting-edge research, knowledge that most people haven't heard about. New research by Dr. Monica Green, for example, now suggests plague was spread not just by traders, but primarily as a result of Mongol sieges in the thirteenth century in places like Iraq, Iran, across the Black Sea region, and into the Mediterranean.

Dr. Jones says, "In the 1340s, this new research also finds evidence of plague north of Iran and Iraq, in Azerbaijan. What links all of these distant places together is Mongol conquest and trade networks, and the rodents that accompanied them (this far west, the plague was probably carried now not by marmots, but by another plague host: rats). The same Mongol link brings us to the Black Sea region, a major trading hub of the time, where plague arrived by 1346."

Now, try showing off your new knowledge with teachers or at home.

Today, the Black Sea is bordered by Ukraine, Romania, Bulgaria, Turkey, Georgia, and Russia. Major rivers flow into it, and ships can pass through the Turkish Straits into the Aegean Sea and the Mediterranean Sea, with access to Italy and other places in Europe. Its central location made it an important place in medieval times—especially to Italian traders.

Let's stop here, in the old city of Caffa. Remember our imaginary merchant from Italy? Caffa was his destination.

PANDEMICS & EPIDEMICS

A **pandemic** is an outbreak of disease that occurs worldwide or over a very large area. It can also continue over a long period of time. An **epidemic** describes the sudden occurrence of cases in a community or population at a particular time. This is also sometimes called an outbreak.

Today, pandemics are officially declared by the United Nation's World Health Organization (**WHO**). WHO is an international agency established in 1948 to bring a global approach to health issues. WHO works to prevent and control health emergencies. It also helps countries prepare for and respond to outbreaks of disease. To learn more about health issues around the globe, visit WHO at who.int.

CHAPTER 2

Old Story, New Evidence

"We were carrying the darts of death . . ."

— GABRIELE DE' MUSSI,
ITALY

People of the medieval era didn't have the internet, shopping malls, or department stores, but they were like us in this way: They enjoyed delicious food and having nice things.

And so, while families and friends waited at home, ambitious Italian merchants from cities like Genoa and Venice traveled much of the globe. As early as 1266, the Genoese established a trading colony in Caffa (also spelled Kaffa), a port on the eastern part of the Crimean peninsula on the Black Sea, sixteen hundred miles from Italy. (Caffa is now Feodosiya, Ukraine.)

Ruins of Caffa Fort on the Black Sea. Today, the city is part of Ukraine.

The Black Sea area has long been part of a large and fruitful grain-growing region. And Caffa was in an ideal location for a brisk trade in rye, wheat, and other staples. Caffa also provided access to other ports like Tana on the Don River, where merchants from both Venice and Genoa traded with the **Golden Horde**, one group of Mongols who controlled parts of Russia and eastern Europe.

Grain was essential to the Italians because they couldn't grow enough themselves. Venice is known for its canals, not its fields. And Genoa is perched on a mountainside. So the Italian merchants needed to bring back rye, wheat, and other staples to feed a growing population back home.

Caffa was well situated for other kinds of trade too. From here, the Italians could mount expeditions to Russia, the Middle East, and China to procure rich silks, furs, spices, and silver. Tragically, the Black Sea region also served as the center for a more horrific form of trade: in enslaved human beings.

The Italians weren't the only ones who saw Caffa's advantages. The Genoese were allowed to operate out of Caffa only because they'd made a deal to buy the city from local **Tatar** leaders. *Tatar* refers to Turkic-speaking tribes and troops of the Golden Horde, the Mongol rulers of Russia and other lands.

With many different groups of people living and working in the Black Sea region, relationships between them were sometimes troubled. And in 1343–1344, Caffa came under attack from a Tatar army. The Tatars surrounded the stone walls of the fortified inner city.

They wanted to starve out the Italians and take control of Caffa. The first siege ended when Italian troops took the upper hand.

But a second siege followed in 1345. The fighting interrupted trade around the Black Sea in 1346. This second siege ended sometime in 1347, and the grain trade got back to normal.

It sounds simple, even a little boring, doesn't it? But these events in the Black Sea region ended up having a huge impact on history.

Mountains of Dead

The siege of Caffa brings us to Gabriele de' Mussi (sometimes spelled Mussis). Gabriele, whose quote begins this chapter, was a notary public in Italy. He created wills and recorded legal documents, like property transactions or loans. Gabriele is one of just a few chroniclers of the Great Mortality in Italy. Historians and writers have often turned to his account of how the disaster began.

And the story Gabriele told about the siege of Caffa is horrendous! Gabriele wrote that when the Tatar army surrounded the inner walls of Caffa, Tatar soldiers started to get sick and die. Then someone hatched a ghastly plan. Bodies of dead soldiers were placed on

Today, as in the past, rats flourish in areas such as grain warehouses and stor bins. Black rats (*Rattus rattus*) infected with plague bacteria were in the grain ships brought to Italy from the Black Sea region in 1347. This picture shows a diffe kind of rat, the Norway rat, *Rattus norvegicus*, in a modern corn storage bin.

catapults and lobbed over the stone walls to poison the air and sicken the Genoese holed up inside the city.

"What seemed like mountains of dead were thrown into the city, and the Christians [Italians] could not hide or flee or escape from them, although they dumped as many of the bodies as they could in the sea," wrote Gabriele. "And soon the rotting corpses tainted the air and poisoned the water supply."

Rotting corpses. Tainted air. Poisoned water. This dramatic story has been repeated in many books about the Great Mortality. But is this really how the Genoese got infected and brought plague back to Italy?

Historians today say no.

Boats, Not Bodies

Professor Hannah Barker is another historian making use of primary sources to look at the past with new eyes. She has studied merchants in the medieval era, including their trade in enslaved people. As part of her research, she has examined primary sources such as diplomatic reports and letters from people who were in the Black Sea region at the time.

One thing struck her about Gabriele de' Mussi's account of the siege of Caffa: He was never there! He got his information secondhand or even thirdhand. So even though his version of events is often used to explain the roots of the Great Mortality, if we look closer we find facts that tell a different story.

As Professor Barker examined documents, a few small details stood out. First, there were no records or mention of plague-infected bodies being catapulted over the walls. In fact, plague spread in a much less dramatic way.

She found evidence that the fighting had interrupted grain shipments in 1346. But when peace came again in 1347, food supplies, including grain, could then be delivered into Caffa. We can guess that rodents also came in with that grain. And, in fact, this is the same pattern researchers like Dr. Green have found in Iran and Iraq, when Mongol sieges ended and plague broke out after grain was brought into cities.

Once the siege ended, the Genoese and Venetians were also able to resume their trade operations in Caffa and the river port of Tana (where there were already reports of plague). They could load up their ships and bring the grain harvest of 1347 back to Italy.

You can already guess what was in those shipments of grain.

Rats. Plague-infected rats.

Darts of Death

Rats live in and around warehouses, docks, and grain storage bins. By the summer of 1347, some rats in the Black Sea region were infected with plague, which had been making its way westward.

Our friend Gabriele *did* get this part of the story right. He wrote, "Some boats were bound for Genoa, others went to Venice and to other . . . areas. When the sailors reached these places and mixed with the people there, it was as if they had brought evil spirits with them: every settlement, every place was poisoned by the **contagious** pestilence, and their inhabitants, both men and women, died suddenly.

"And when one person had contracted the illness, he poisoned his whole family even as he fell and died, so that those preparing to bury his body were seized by death in the same way." The sailors were carrying "the darts of death."

The darts of death.

Gabriele couldn't have described it any better. Because when a rat dies of plague, its fleas look around for some other warm body to feed on—and people have warm bodies.

When those fleas bite, they leave behind a microscopic bacterium, so tiny it's impossible to see with the naked eye. That bite is a dart of death.

It's time to meet *Yersinia pestis*.

OTHER NAMES FOR THE GREAT MORTALITY

Medieval chroniclers in Europe referred to the terrible outbreak that struck Italy beginning in late 1347 as the Big Death, the Great Dying, the Pestilence, or the Great Mortality. In Europe, the disease spread from Italy into Spain, France, and Germany, and at the same time made its way by ship to England, Wales, Scotland, and Ireland. During this time, plague was also spreading through the Middle East and North Africa, affecting societies in Greece, Azerbaijan, Armenia, Syria, Iraq, and elsewhere.

Scholars usually use 1346 or 1347 as the beginning of the Great Mortality. And while there are various dates used to mark its end, plague seems to have died out after an outbreak in Moscow, Russia, in 1353.

The Deadliest Diseases Then and Now

You may be familiar with one of the most common nicknames for the plague of this period in European history: the "Black Death." Some people assume the name Black Death was around in the 1300s because of some of the symptoms of the disease. **Septicemic plague** can cause tissue to die and turn black.

However, the term *Black Death* wasn't used by our on-the-spot chroniclers or people living at the time. It actually came about when a seventeenth-century historian *claimed* the phrase had been in use in medieval times. It soon became the common name to describe the outbreak.

Here, we'll follow the lead of our primary sources and use the Great Mortality. It's also your chance to show off your new knowledge of history—and explain why chroniclers like us prefer to call it the Great Mortality.

When scientists have examined ancient teeth, they've found evidence that humans suffered from plague as far back as the Neolithic period, roughly five thousand years ago. We'll never know how widespread it was then, or how many it killed. But in recorded history, medical historians have counted three major plague pandemics.

- **First Pandemic (6th to 8th centuries), beginning with the Plague of Justinian.** In 542, plague arrived in the city of Constantinople. It was then part of the Eastern Roman Empire ruled by Emperor Justinian. This pandemic likely killed at least twenty-five million people. One account says five thousand people died each day in Constantinople, where the disease raged for four months.

- **Second Pandemic (14th to 19th centuries).** The Second Pandemic was launched with the Great Mortality, the sudden, catastrophic unleashing of plague in Europe, the Middle East, and North

A woman carrying a child's coffin during a plague outbreak.
Lithograph by Felix Jenewein, 1900. Note the use of face coverings.

Africa. In Europe, it decimated populations in Italy, France, and Britain. Although we don't have enough evidence to know the actual number of deaths, some historians estimate that between 40 and 60 percent of the population died. Sporadic outbreaks of plague continued to occur in western Europe for hundreds of years after the Great Mortality. Some historians mark the Great Plague of Marseille in 1720–1722 as the end of the Second Pandemic in Europe. However, severe plague outbreaks continued to devastate North Africa, Russia, and other areas throughout the eighteenth and nineteenth centuries.

- **Third Pandemic (1855–1960).** Scholars also assign various dates to the Third Pandemic. In fact, the boundaries between the Second Pandemic and the Third Pandemic are so blurred, it's not really possible to say when one ended and the other began. Often, the beginning of the Third Pandemic is traced to the 1850s in China. Plague outbreaks then spread worldwide, affecting numerous port cities such as Calcutta (now Kolkata), Bombay (today Mumbai), Hong Kong, Bangkok, Cape Town, and San Francisco. Although exact figures can't be known, some historians estimate that by 1922 the Third Pandemic may have killed ten to fifteen million people, many in India.

CHAPTER 3

Meet Y. pestis: Hosts, Vectors, People

"'It is of the form of an apple, like the head of an onion, a small boil that spares no one. Great is its seething, like a burning cinder, a grievous thing of an ashy color.'"

— JEUAN GETHIN,
WALES

The common cold, flu, and COVID-19 are caused by viruses. Plague, like cholera, tuberculosis, and pneumonia, is a bacterial disease. Plague is caused by a rod-shaped **bacillus** called *Yersinia pestis*. It's often abbreviated *Y. pestis*. It gets its name from Alexandre Yersin, one of the men who discovered it. We'll find out more about him later.

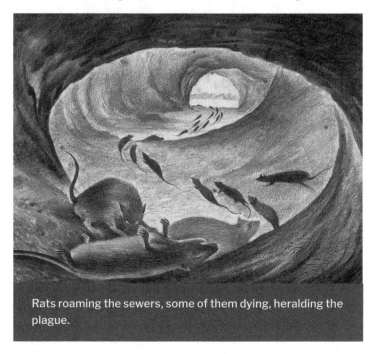

Rats roaming the sewers, some of them dying, heralding the plague.

While we often connect plague with marmots and rats, *Y. pestis* can infect many different **species** of animals. Prairie dogs, wild gerbils, camels, hares, mice, squirrels, chipmunks, voles, coyotes, and even dogs and cats can get plague.

Luckily, in most of the world, large outbreaks of plague are extremely rare. However, some areas still see regular cases.

BINOMIAL SYSTEM

L ike other organisms, *Y. pestis* is named according to the **binomial system** developed by Carl Linnaeus (1707–1778). The binomial system gives each living thing a unique name.

In this system, the organism name includes the **genus** and species. A genus is a small group of organisms that are closely related; a species is a group of similar individuals capable of breeding with one another. In the case of *Yersinia pestis*, *Yersinia* is the genus and the species is known as *Y. pestis*. Another related bacterium in the same genus is *Yersinia pseudotuberculosis* or *Y. pseudotuberculosis*. In another example, within the genus *Panthera*, we have the species *P. tigris* (tiger) and also the species *P. leo* (lion).

In central Asia, this happens because there's a natural reservoir of plague in marmots, burrowing rodents that live in large numbers in underground burrows in the high grasslands of the steppe. Marmots have long been hunted for fur, skin (for leather), and meat—and they continue to be hunted in Mongolia, a country that sits between Russia and China. There have been recent plague outbreaks in the island country of Madagascar, an island nation in the Indian Ocean off the coast of east Africa.

Cases of plague also occur regularly in the Southwest United States, where plague bacteria live naturally in prairie dog populations. It's important to avoid wild animals, treat household pets for fleas, and take sick dogs and cats to the vet. If you live in an area where there are prairie dogs, don't let your own dog loose to hunt or roam.

A reservoir of plague means plague bacteria circulate at a low rate in populations of rodents without causing problems for people. No one knows exactly how it circulates in the wild, though scientists believe plague bacteria may survive in the soil of the burrows of marmots, prairie dogs, and other rodents. Some animals may develop resistance to the bacteria.

However, sometimes there is a large outbreak in an animal population. An epidemic of disease in animals is called an epizootic. Scientists believe that plague epizootics are when the disease is most likely to jump over into humans. Hunters, for instance, are more likely to come in contact with infected marmots. Also, during a plague epizootic, many animals die. Hungry fleas need other sources of blood. Without their animal hosts, fleas may turn to farm animals or humans.

Marmots are most likely the original source of plague outbreaks in Asia in the thirteenth and fourteenth centuries. But plague found other animal hosts too. After all, marmots didn't travel in the caravans of traders. They didn't live close to villages, docks, or places where grain was stored. They didn't stow away on ships. Rats did.

Y. pestis + Rats + Fleas

In medieval times, black rats (*Rattus rattus*) were often found living near humans. Rats ate the same food as people, including rye and wheat. They were plentiful near grain storage bins and on ships. However, people didn't catch plague from rats directly.

That's because plague is a **zoonotic disease**. That means people get it from an infected animal by means of an agent, or vector. (Lyme disease is another example of a zoonotic disease. It spreads from small mammals or birds to humans via ticks.)

Vectors are living organisms that transmit infectious pathogens (organisms that can cause disease) between humans, or from animals to humans. Vectors are often bloodsucking insects. And for plague, that vector is usually a flea.

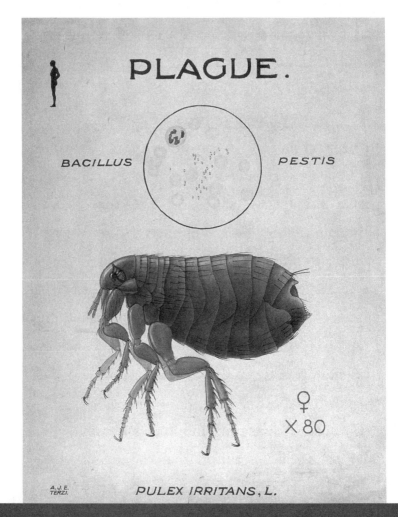

Spores of Bacillus *pestis* (*Yersinia pestis*), which causes the plague, and its vector the human flea (*Pulex irritans*). Human fleas, like rat fleas, serve as vectors for plague. Researchers now believe that body lice probably served as vectors for plague during the Great Mortality too.

ABOUT BACTERIA

Four billion years ago, bacteria emerged as the first simple forms of life on Earth. These single-cell **microbes**, or **microorganisms**, are so tiny they can be seen only through a microscope. Microbes include bacteria, fungi, and **protists** like algae. (Although viruses are also small, they don't technically fall into the category of microorganisms. That's because they don't have cells, so are usually considered nonliving.)

Bacteria are found everywhere, from deep in the ocean to inside the human body and even in space. The singular of *bacteria* is *bacterium*.

Scientists put bacteria into five categories, depending on their shape. *Yersinia pestis* is rod-shaped. A single rod-shaped bacterium can also be called a bacillus. (Bacilli would be more than one.) The five categories of bacteria are:

—Spherical (cocci)

—Rod (bacilli)

—Spiral (spirilla)

—Comma (vibrios)

—Corkscrew (spirochetes)

Before scientists could see bacteria under a microscope, they suspected some kind of "little creatures" must exist. Using primitive microscopes, Robert Hooke described the fruiting structures of molds in 1665 and also helped scientists understand that microorganisms can cause infectious diseases. Antonie van Leeuwenhoek is credited with the discovery of bacteria in 1676.

Rat Fleas: A Powerful Plague Delivery System

Although scientists have found that plague can be transmitted by human fleas (*Pulex irritans*) and body lice (*Pediculus humanus humanus*), its most common vector has been the Oriental rat flea (*Xenopsylla cheopis*).

Rat fleas and human fleas have different habits. Human fleas spend more time off their hosts. They might, for instance, nest in bedding, textiles, or clothing. This behavior makes them nest fleas. By contrast, rat fleas are host fleas. They like to spend all their lives on their host.

It's only when a plague-infected rat dies and its body grows cold that rat fleas look for another warm-blooded creature on which to feed. And *Y. pestis* has evolved a devious way of making sure rat fleas infect this new host. The fleas become **blocked**.

It works like this: When a flea bites a rat, it takes in blood and bacteria. This forms a sticky ball inside the flea's gut. Fleas have several parts to their stomachs; this ball gets stuck inside one part called the foregut, or proventriculus.

This sticky ball can't be digested. The flea keeps feeling hungrier and hungrier because it's blocked. But that just makes it want to keep eating. And each time it bites, it spits up plague bacteria and blood into the new host.

This doesn't end well for anyone—except the plague germ. Because no matter how much it tries to eat, the flea ends up starving to death since it can't digest anything. However, before it dies, it has passed on the plague bacteria quite effectively. In other words, *Y. pestis* has made the rat flea the perfect partner in its quest to infect organisms.

The next three photos show how this happens inside a rat flea.

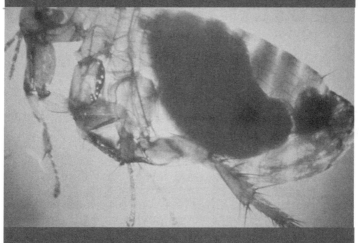

This image depicts a magnified left lateral view of an Oriental rat flea, *Xenopsylla cheopis*. At this point, the flea's stomach and proventriculus remain unblocked, though it has just fed upon an infected host's blood, which forms a dark cloud that can be seen inside its gut.

Here, the flea's stomach and proventriculus are still unblocked. However, the future **blockage** has begun to form inside its stomach, which is visible as a darkening mass. This dark spot is made up of plague bacteria.

In this third view, the flea's stomach and proventriculus are completely blocked by a mass of *Yersinia pestis* bacteria.

Y. pestis + Rats + Fleas + People

The human toll in Europe, the Middle East, and Africa during the Great Mortality was almost unthinkable, with up to 60 percent of the population perishing. The high death toll has led some scientists to wonder if plague was the only disease to blame. Along with plague, it's quite likely some people died from other diseases and from malnutrition and lack of food.

Finding evidence from so long ago isn't always easy

or possible—but the lack of evidence doesn't mean something didn't occur. For example, if the Great Mortality was caused by **bubonic plague** carried by rat fleas, we might expect to find evidence of "rat falls," large dying-offs of rats. Archaeologists haven't found physical evidence of rat falls—yet, at least. But rat bones are tiny and simply may not have survived. Or perhaps other rodents or domesticated farm animals played a part, especially in the countryside. They became hosts, and when they died, their fleas also turned to people.

We can point to other clues as to how plague spread so rapidly during the Great Mortality. First, it seems people passed the disease quickly from one to another. This suggests that in addition to rat fleas, human fleas and body lice served as vectors as well.

One thing is certain: Historians and scientists will continue to uncover new evidence about the Great Mortality and how it affected the world. And that's what makes learning and research so exciting.

Same Disease: Three Common Forms

There's another reason so many people died during the Great Mortality. It has to do with the disease itself and why it spread so quickly. There is more than one type of plague. We've already heard of bubonic plague. This is the most common form, and it attacks the lymph nodes. There are other types of plague too, some quite rare. Along with bubonic plague, the other two most common forms are **pneumonic plague**, which infects the lungs, and septicemic plague, which targets the bloodstream. Here's a brief look at each.

Bubonic Plague: This is the most common and "mildest" version of plague. People get it after being bitten by a vector, such as a flea or louse. Inside the victim's body, the bacilli travel through the bloodstream and replicate in the lymph nodes. The nodes swell and become painful bulges, called buboes. Sometimes they burst and discharge pus. Patients also can experience fever, headache, weakness, and chills.

During past plague pandemics, about 30 to 60 percent of bubonic plague victims died. Today, especially if caught early, bubonic plague can be treated successfully with antibiotics such as streptomycin. Only about 2 percent of cases are fatal.

Pneumonic Plague: Pneumonic plague is the most contagious form of the disease. It's possible to get pneumonic plague in two ways.

Secondary Pneumonic Plague: Someone who has bubonic plague first can end up with the bacilli attacking their lungs as well as their lymph nodes. This leads to secondary pneumonic plague. Patients experience fever, headache, and weakness, along with shortness of breath. Pneumonia develops rapidly and death follows.

Primary Pneumonic Plague: The rosy sputum coughed up by someone with secondary pneumonic plague isn't contagious at first. But soon the patient begins coughing up more blood full of bacteria. This can spew into the air and infect others with primary pneumonic plague. In this case, the plague germ goes straight to the lungs, not the lymph nodes. Buboes won't form. In the past, this was 100 percent fatal. Antibiotics must be given within the first twenty-four hours or it may cause death.

Septicemic Plague: In this rare form of plague, the plague bacilli enter a person's bloodstream, causing a massive infection. This form of plague can be a complication of pneumonic plague or it can be caused the same way as bubonic plague, but there are no buboes. In some cases, death can occur within a day.

In septicemic plague, a victim's circulation can be affected. When the blood supply fails to reach tissue, cells die. This can cause some parts of the body, especially the extremities, like fingers and toes, to become hard and black. Septicemic plague is not spread from person to person.

As we shall see next from our medieval chroniclers, during the Great Mortality, people in Europe suffered horribly from both bubonic and pneumonic plague. Remarkably, even without real medical knowledge about plague, some observers at the time realized these were various forms of the same disease. These chroniclers provide useful information for understanding how the disease spread so fast.

No matter the form it takes, plague is a sneaky disease. If you've ever hurt yourself, you might sometimes see that your skin is red around the cut. That's a sign of inflammation, which triggers your body's immune response to fight against infection. When *Y. pestis* enters the body, it doesn't cause an inflammatory reaction. It's like an invisible enemy sneaking in for the attack. By the time symptoms appear, the bacteria have already been multiplying furiously, taking over.

That's why, even now, anyone with a suspected case of plague is urged to get treatment immediately. But don't worry—luckily, in the United States, plague is very rare. Even so, it's always a good idea to keep your distance from wild creatures.

CHAPTER 4

The Great Mortality Strikes Italy

"They brought with them a plague that they carried down to the very marrow of their bones . . ."

— MICHELE DA PIAZZA
(MICHAEL OF PIAZZA),
ITALY

It's easy to imagine the joy medieval sailors would have felt returning home to Italy in the fall of 1347. Photographs of the old-town section of Genoa hint at its colorful seafaring past. Ships and sailboats bob in the harbor. People stroll through piazzas and gather in cafés. Picturesque alleyways snake up hillsides dotted with pink and cream houses.

The long journey from the Black Sea would have begun in late August, once ships were loaded with the

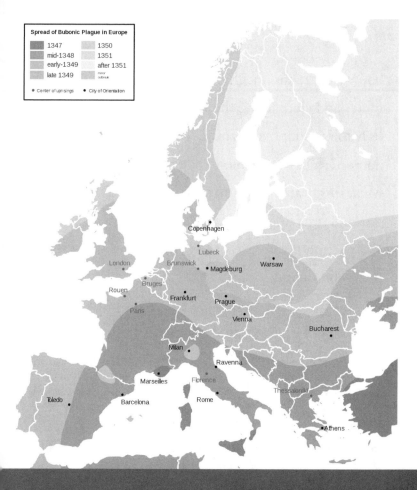

Spread of Bubonic Plague in Europe

1347
mid-1348
early-1349
late 1349
1350
1351
after 1351
minor outbreak

● Center of uprisings ● City of Orientation

Copenhagen
Lubeck
London
Brunswick
Bruges
Magdeburg
Warsaw
Rouen
Frankfurt
Paris
Prague
Vienna
Bucharest
Milan
Ravenna
Marseilles
Florence
Thessaloniki
Toledo
Barcelona
Rome
Athens

This map shows how plague came to Europe, but that was only one part of the world affected by plague in the mid-1300s. Historians are continuing to do research that will help develop new maps based on evidence to better show the entire scope of the outbreak, which affected Central Asia, the Middle East, North Africa, and perhaps Sub-Saharan Africa too.

In this map, east of Bucharest is the Black Sea, with the Crimean peninsula visible at the far right edge of the map. Caffa sits on the southeast part of that peninsula.

bounty of the summer harvest. Depending on shipping routes and stops along the way, the trip from Caffa to Italy took about two months. That fall, of course, those doomed ships carried more than grain. What happened when this deadly cargo arrived?

Let's hear from some of the Italian chroniclers who left an unforgettable record of the disaster that turned their world upside down.

The Plague Arrives in Sicily

Our first eyewitness is Michele da Piazza, known in English as Michael of Piazza. Michael was a Franciscan friar in Sicily, the island that forms the toe of Italy's boot. He lived in a monastery in Catania, a city not far from Messina, where twelve Genoese ships put into harbor in October of 1347.

We know medieval ships visited a network of trading stations and ports along the way. There would be stops to trade and stock up on water and food. It's likely that if crew members got sick and died at sea, others would have been found to take their place. And by the time the Genoese ships reached Messina, plague was sweeping through the crew.

"They brought with them a plague that they carried down to the very marrow of their bones," wrote Michael, "so that if anyone so much as spoke to them, he was infected with a mortal sickness which brought on an immediate death that he could in no way avoid."

The plague jumped quickly from ship to shore. Michael described people suffering from both bubonic and pneumonic plague. It's instantly clear this disease was extremely contagious.

He wrote that "victims violently coughed up blood, and after three days' incessant vomiting, for which there was no remedy, they died—and with them died not only anyone who had talked with them, but also anyone who had acquired or touched or laid hands on their belongings."

The city took action. "The people of Messina, realizing that the death racing through them was linked with the arrival of the Genoese galleys [ships that are propelled mainly by rowing], expelled the Genoese from the city and harbor with all speed," Michael reported.

"But the illness remained in the city and subsequently caused enormous mortality," wrote Michael. "Not just one person in a house died, but the whole household, down to the cats and the livestock, followed their master to death."

Even the cats and the livestock. Plague had arrived— and there was no way to stop it.

Plague Unleashed

Weeks later, other ships returning from Caffa reached their home port of Genoa in the north of Italy. Plague raced inland here too. As cloth, flour, and rye grain were shipped to towns in carts and wagons, rats and fleas went along. And, of course, people themselves carried fleas and body lice wherever they went.

By the spring of 1348, the Great Mortality had a

firm toehold in Italy. It unleashed unspeakable fear, panic, confusion, and heartbreak.

Our chronicler friend Gabriele de' Mussi lived in Piacenza, about a hundred miles from Genoa. Gabriele realized he was witnessing a tumultuous time, though he probably never imagined anyone would be reading his words so many centuries later.

But Gabriele certainly understood the value of being an eyewitness to history. "Everyone has a responsibility to keep some record of the disease and deaths," he wrote, adding, "so that the conditions, causes and symptoms of the pestilential disease should be made plain to all, I have decided to set them out in writing."

Gabriele told of a man who fled Genoa for safety and stayed with a family in another town. But it seems the man had brought some merchandise with him. The entire household and neighbors became infected, most likely as a result of plague-infected fleas hidden in cloth.

"One man there, wanting to make his will, died

along with the notary, the priest who heard his confession, and the people summoned to witness the will, and they were all buried together on the following day," Gabriele tells us.

Today, health care workers and religious leaders who visit the sick in hospitals are especially prone to getting infected. The same was true then. Gabriele recounts the horrors of entire families being struck down with the disease, and the heartbreak of having no cure or treatment.

"Priests and doctors, upon whom most of the care of the sick devolved, had their hands full in visiting the sick and, alas, by the time they left they too had been infected and followed the dead immediately to the grave."

Getting Plague: A Fearsome Attack

People living in Italy at that time had never experienced plague before. It must have been terrifying to see family members fall ill, fearing you might be next. Gabriele tells us exactly what happened when people got sick. His words allow us to imagine what it was like to watch a loved one die of plague.

"First, out of the blue, a kind of chilly stiffness troubled their bodies. They felt a tingling sensation, as if they were being pricked by the points of arrows.

"The next stage was a fearsome attack which took the form of an extremely hard, solid boil [bubo or buboes]. In some people this developed under the armpit and in others in the groin . . . As it grew more solid, its burning heat caused the patients to fall into an acute and putrid fever, with severe headaches."

Shocked and scared, everyone wondered why this was happening. Gabriele had an idea: "Behold the swellings, the warning signs sent by the Lord."

A Punishment from God

Gabriele wasn't alone in thinking the Great Mortality was a punishment sent by an angry God. During the coronavirus pandemic in 2020, communities around the world could rely on scientists, facts, and experts trained in public health.

But in fourteenth-century Europe, doctors didn't know that diseases were caused by germs, or pathogens, too small to see, such as bacteria and viruses. This evidence-based understanding of how diseases spread, known as **germ theory**, wasn't fully accepted until the late 1800s.

Dr. Lori Jones tells us more about medical knowledge at the time. She explains that "doctors could not know about germs or pathogens because microscopes had not been invented yet. Instead, they based their understanding of disease on a different understanding of the world around them.

"First, they believed that there was a connection between all things on earth and in the skies. Certain alignments of the planets or earthquakes were thought to poison the air, and if breathed in, this air could poison people and animals. Second, the air could also be poisoned by **miasma**, the rotten smells that came from garbage or stagnant water (think about how we today still associate bad smells with danger!).

"Third, people's bodies could become imbalanced on the inside. While doctors did not talk very much about warnings from God, religious leaders did, and many blamed the plague on people's sinful ways."

Sometimes during the Great Mortality, fear, prejudice, and ignorance also led to blaming others. And, as we'll see in the next chapter, there were horrific incidents of **antisemitism** and violence against the Jewish community, especially in central Europe.

Medieval Remedies and Practices

Just like the twenty-first century when people faced a new coronavirus, those living during the Great Mortality tried their best to stay healthy and keep from getting sick. Much of what they did was based on practices followed at the time—and a dose of common sense. Here are some remedies they tried:

- Shutting windows in order to keep out danger-ous "bad air," and fumigating houses by burning incense or fragrant wood, such as pine.
- Making healthy drinks containing cider, vinegar, and spices like cloves and rosemary.
- Carrying flowers to keep the stench away.
- Keeping the body in balance by living a healthy lifestyle. And just like now, that included eating well and getting enough sleep and exercise.
- Bloodletting, using a small lance to draw off "bad blood."
- Lancing the buboes of bubonic plague or treating them with ointments.

None of these remedies could cure a bacterial ill-ness, of course. But some practices might have helped reduce its spread. For example, many towns ordered that streets be cleaned, garbage be collected, cesspits be emptied, water channels be cleared, and new cemeter-ies be built outside the city walls.

Town residents were ordered to keep the ditches clean and weren't allowed to throw garbage into the streets. The towns formed committees to help regulate the cloth trade, and banned animals and butchers in town centers. They also oversaw the destruction of clothing and bedding of infected people. Finally, they put strict new rules in place about where people could gather and go. They changed how funerals took place, for example.

Isolating the sick and keeping away from others helped people avoid the disease. Today, we call keeping space between ourselves and others physical distancing, sometimes called social distancing. Isolating at home or in a separate facility and not going out is being in **quarantine**.

With the Speed of a Fire

We know some details of the plague in Florence, Italy, thanks to Giovanni Boccaccio (1313–1375). Giovanni wrote one of the most famous books about the Great

Mortality, called *The Decameron*. It's a collection of one hundred tales, told by ten fictional characters who have fled to a villa outside Florence to escape plague. They keep themselves occupied by sharing stories. The book is fiction, but in the introduction, Giovanni includes his own observations of life in Florence in the spring of 1348. Although historians note that he exaggerated a lot, his words remind us of how frightening it must have been to confront a disease as contagious as plague.

"But what made this pestilence even more severe was that whenever those suffering from it mixed with people who were still unaffected, it would rush upon those with the speed of a fire racing through dry or oily substances that happened to be placed within its reach," Giovanni wrote.

No one knew what to do. Giovanni reported that some people tried to form their own groups and live together in isolation. "They refrained from speaking to outsiders, refused to receive news of the dead or sick, and entertained themselves with music and whatever other amusement they were able to devise."

Others ran away, abandoning their families, homes—and even their children. Still others, Giovanni said, stayed where they were, determined to defy the sickness. They tried to enjoy life fully, singing and eating and visiting taverns.

In the end, it didn't seem to matter much.

"In the face of its onrush, all the wisdom and ingenuity of man were unavailing," Giovanni wrote. "Large quantities of refuse were cleared out of the city by officials specially appointed for the purpose, all sick persons were forbidden entry, and numerous instructions were issued for safeguarding the people's health, but all to no avail."

Nothing could stop the Great Mortality.

Just a First Stop

The plague devastated Italy in the spring and summer of 1348, although its ferociousness lessened in 1349.

Most experts estimate that at least 30 to 40 percent of the population died. In 2017, some scholars who examined local records put the mortality rate in Florence even higher, at 60 percent.

But Italy was just the first stop. Plague was already making its way north, into France and central Europe. There it would unleash not only death from disease, but waves of violence against the Jewish community.

CHAPTER 5

Death by Disease and Hate

"And I call the mortality great because it overtook the whole world, or nearly all of it."

— GUY DE CHAULIAC,
FRANCE

I f time travel ever becomes a real thing, take my advice: Don't choose 1348. It may well have been one of the most terrible years to have been alive.

By that spring, plague had taken hold in Italy and was already breaking out in France and other countries in central Europe. While there are many places we could visit in order to tell the story of plague in central Europe, let's stop in Avignon, in southeastern France. You may know that Rome is the center of the Roman

Catholic Church. However, for nearly seventy years in the 1300s, popes made Avignon, France, their home instead.

During the Great Mortality, Clement VI (1291–1352) served as the pope. His personal physician was Guy (sometimes Gui) de Chauliac. Dr. Chauliac lived from 1300 until 1368. And while you may never have heard of him, if this remarkable doctor hadn't survived the plague, the history of medicine might have been quite different.

Dr. Chauliac was from a poor family, but he was able to study medicine through a scholarship. In 1325, he received a Master of medicine from the University of Montpellier in France. It's hard to imagine undergoing an operation without pain-killing anesthesia, but Dr. Chauliac was determined to improve people's lives through surgery. He was successful in using opium or herb mixtures to put people to sleep during simple surgeries, such as fractures. Dr. Chauliac's medical training also made him a careful observer and valuable chronicler of the Great Mortality in France.

Like Shooting Arrows

Dr. Chauliac tells us the outbreak in Avignon began in January of 1348 and lasted seven months. In the first two months, it seems that pneumonic plague may have been responsible for the rapid spread of the disease. For example, in describing symptoms, Dr. Chauliac notes that those who fell ill experienced "continuous fever and a spitting up of blood, and one died within three days."

Dr. Chauliac's description gives us a chilling sense of what this time was like. He writes, "And the mortality was so contagious, especially in those who were spitting up blood, that not only did one get it from another by living together, but also by looking at each other, to the point that people died without servants and were buried without priests. The father did not visit his son, nor the son his father; charity was dead, hope crushed.

"And I call the mortality great because it overtook the whole world, or nearly all of it. But it began in the

East, and like shooting arrows it passed through us on its way west. And it was so great that it hardly left a quarter of the human race."

All of My Friends Believed I Would Die

Dr. Chauliac's role as personal physician to the pope was an important one. Even if he had wanted to flee, he didn't feel he could: His reputation as a leading doctor of his time was on the line. Fortunately, he advised Pope Clement VI to isolate himself in a room with two fires burning. This isolation most likely saved the pope's life.

But Dr. Chauliac himself didn't escape the disease. Luckily, he contracted the milder form, bubonic plague, at the tail end of the outbreak. "Nonetheless, toward the end of the mortality I fell into a continuous fever, with an aposteme [abscess; swelling filled with pus] on the groin, and I was sick for nearly six weeks. And I was in such great danger that all of my friends believed I would die."

Dr. Chauliac survived to publish his *Chirugia Magna*, or "great work on surgery." It was written in Latin in 1363 and was used by doctors for at least two hundred years. Dr. Chauliac's guiding words for his fellow physicians, entitled "What the Surgeon Ought to Be," called for surgeons to be learned, expert, ingenious, and flexible—principles still valued by medical professionals today.

Hatred Unleashed: Persecution of Jews

Dr. Chauliac was a keen medical observer. He also recorded one of the most disturbing aspects of the Great Mortality. Driven by fear, ignorance, suspicion, and racial hatred, some people tried to find scapegoats. They wanted someone to blame. This led to the violent persecution of Jews in 1348 and 1349 in central Europe as well as in France, Spain, and Belgium.

"Many were uncertain about the cause of this great mortality. In some places, they believed that the Jews had poisoned the world, and so they killed them," Dr. Chauliac reported.

Jewish people suffered from antisemitism and violent attacks during the Great Mortality. Antisemitism is prejudice, persecution, or racial hatred directed at Jewish people.

In some places, Jews were accused of poisoning wells to unleash plague. Mob violence reigned; anti-Jewish riots broke out. People launched violent attacks, called **pogroms**, against Jewish communities. Jewish families weren't safe in their homes.

The attacks were motivated by prejudice, and also greed. At this time, Christians weren't allowed to lend money and charge interest on loans (the way banks do today if someone wants to buy a car or house). But Jews could be moneylender. The pogroms enabled Christian people to erase their debts and steal from the Jewish community. The Great Mortality was simply used as an excuse to persecute and rob.

One of the most horrific attacks was the massacre in Strasbourg (now in eastern France) on February 14, 1349. Hundreds of Jews were burned to death. Many others were chased from town, losing their homes and belongings. Many thousands of innocent Jewish people in France, Germany, Austria, and Switzerland were killed in attacks like these.

In most cases, political and religious leaders did very little to stop the violence and restore order. Acts of violence against Jews continued until around 1351, when the worst of the plague outbreak in Europe was over.

CONFRONT BULLYING BEHAVIOR: BECOME AN UPSTANDER!

Everyone deserves respect and to be treated with kindness. Acts of racial hatred, prejudice, and antisemitism often begin as bullying. And they can happen in school or on the playground.

You are not powerless. You can take action to stand up to bullying or meanness. If you are being bullied, you can ask a grown-up you trust for help.

To learn safe strategies, visit "What Kids Can Do" at the United States government's Stop Bullying website at https://www.stopbullying.gov/resources/kids.

CHAPTER 6

Across the Narrow Sea

"It is seething, terrible, wherever it may come . . ."

— JEUAN GETHIN,
WALES

Fourteen-year-old Princess Joan of England must have felt excited. It was the summer of 1348 and she was about to become a bride. The young princess set out from England on her way to Castile (now part of Spain) to marry a prince.

The princess had so many retainers and servants, it took four ships to convey the royal party. Princess Joan had brought gifts, clothes, and furnishings for her new home, including an elegant silk wedding dress, elaborate riding outfits, and ornate bed curtains.

But even a rich, well-protected princess wasn't safe

from plague. When the travelers stopped in France, Princess Joan fell sick. She never got the chance to wear her gorgeous wedding dress. She died from plague, becoming one of the first English victims.

She wouldn't be the last.

A Toehold in England

Plague's arrival in England is often traced to two ships that docked in late June of 1348 at the harbor of Melcombe Regis. It's now part of the seaside town of Weymouth in southern England. England is separated from northern France by the English Channel; back then, it was simply known as the Narrow Sea.

But as we know from our detective work on Italy, it's very likely plague entered England on a number of ships that summer. It was the best season for trading ships to operate—milder weather meant safer travels. By August, plague was reported in Ireland too.

Just as it had in Italy, the disease may have begun at the seaside, but it soon fanned out, spreading to towns and villages, hopping and skipping its way inland as traders moved with their goods from one place to another. Fear spread along with it. As rumors flew, church leaders shared prayers to be recited by the faithful.

"There can be no one who does not know, since it is now public knowledge, how great a mortality, pestilence and infection of the air are now threatening various parts of the world, and especially England; and this is surely caused by the sins of men," wrote the Archbishop of York.

By October, plague had reached London. In mid-November, King Edward III ordered the port of London closed.

It was far too late.

The Great Mortality in London

London was founded as Londinium when the Romans arrived in England in 43 CE, early in the first century. London sits on the Thames, a busy river then and now.

The Deadliest Diseases Then and Now

Artist's sketch of a woman sitting above a makeshift grave with plague victims.

During the mid-1300s, about seventy-five thousand people lived in this crowded city.

One useful primary source for historians studying the plague in London is wills. Unlike today, people back then didn't usually make a will until they were on their deathbeds. Since records show an increase in the number of wills in the fall of 1348, we know plague had begun to take a toll in London.

Other evidence comes from burial grounds. As more people died, the question soon became: Where to put the bodies? London officials arranged for three new burial grounds outside the city walls. One was quite large: thirteen acres.

"This pestilence held such sway in England at that time that there were hardly enough people left alive to bury the dead, or enough burial grounds to hold them . . . The pestilence grew so strong that men and women dropped dead while walking in the streets," said Thomas Burton, an English monk. He was writing about the plague several decades later and so probably didn't see these things with his own eyes, but his words show us how the stories of the plague took hold in people's minds.

The Great Mortality hit London hard. While we don't have exact numbers, we know thousands of lives were lost. When the worst was over, people must have breathed a sigh of relief. But as we'll see in the next chapter, plague wasn't done with London. Not by any means.

The Sad Chronicle of Friar Clynn

We've come to our last chronicler of the Great Mortality, and his story is the saddest. His name was John Clynn; he was born around 1300, the same year as Dr. Chauliac in France. John Clynn was a Franciscan friar, or monk. He compiled a history of Ireland, and left us the only record there is of the Great Mortality in Ireland.

"It first began near Dublin, at Howth, and at Drogheda, and virtually wiped out those cities, emptying them of inhabitants," he wrote. "In Dublin alone

14,000 people died between the beginning of August and Christmas [1348]. This pestilence was said to have arisen in the east and to have killed some forty million people."

Friar Clynn's words help us see how frightening it must have been for people to see so many of their friends, family, and neighbors snatched away by this terrible disease—yet feel so powerless to do anything to help.

"Since the beginning of the world it has been unheard of for so many people to die of pestilence, famine or other infirmity in such a short time . . . Plague stripped villages, cities, castles and towns of their inhabitants so thoroughly that there was scarcely anyone alive in them.

"This pestilence was so contagious that those who touched the dead or the sick were immediately infected themselves and died, so that penitent and confessor were carried to the grave. Because of their fear and horror, men could hardly bring themselves to perform the pious and charitable acts of visiting the sick and bury-ing the dead."

We're not sure if Friar Clynn himself comforted families or visited the sick. We know many priests as well as doctors did just that—and they caught the disease and died. Like Dr. Chauliac in France, Friar Clynn fell ill with plague. He wasn't as lucky as Dr. Chauliac, however, and may already have guessed his fate when he wrote these last words.

"And I, Brother John Clynn, of the Friars Minor of Kilkenny, have written in this book the notable events which befell in my time, which I saw for myself or have learnt from men worthy of belief.

"So that notable deeds should not perish with time, and be lost from the memory of future generations, I . . . have committed to writing what I have truly heard and examined; and so that the writing does not perish with the writer, or the work fail with the work-man, I leave parchment for continuing the work, in case anyone should still be alive in the future and any son of Adam can escape this pestilence and continue the work thus begun."

No one added to his story. But another monk, copying it out later, added these words, "Here it seems the author died." Friar John Clynn died of plague in 1349.

Etching of two plague victims and a baby who is still alive during the great plague outbreak of 1665 in London.

Part Two

PLAGUE, PLAGUE, AND MORE PLAGUE

"'The world is changed and overthrown . . .'"

— UNKNOWN POET

CHAPTER 7

Waves of Plague in a World Transformed

"'But it was not only in the Year 1665 that Plague raged in London, we have Accounts in the Bills of Mortality [death records], of that dreadful Distemper in the Years 1592, 1603, 1625, 1630, and 1635 . . .'"

— RICHARD BRADLEY, LONDON

Victims of the plague in 1665 being lifted onto death carts.

Waves of Plague in a World Transformed

The Great Mortality in Europe lasted until about 1353, when the disease spread east to Russia, where it seems to have died out. It left behind millions of shaken and stunned survivors. Families tried to put their lives back together and make sense of what had happened. With from 40 to 60 percent of the population dead, no family in Europe was left untouched by grief and sadness.

If you had become an orphan in Genoa, Italy, you might have lost your fine house. Perhaps, before she died, your mother was able to arrange for a relative to care for you and your brother. She might have made a will and left you some money, enough for you to open a shop.

If you'd been a peasant in the English countryside, you might have found work as a servant in a manor house. You would have been paid more than before the Great Mortality: Servants were now hard to find. If you worked the land, you would have been able to sell your vegetables and grain for higher prices.

You and any of your family who survived might have been able to rent more land, and perhaps buy a small farm for the first time. If you grew up and married, you might have been able to expand your farm and even pass on land to your own children.

No matter what, your life would have been forever changed by the Great Mortality.

A World Upside Down

The Great Mortality and the deaths of so many left a mark on families, communities, and on society as a whole. In the words of an unnamed poet:

> *"The world is changed and overthrown*
> *That is well-nigh upside down*
> *Compared with days of long ago."*

In medieval Europe, the landholding class was at the top. Nobles and the wealthy owned most of the land, which was worked by poor peasants or tenant farmers. This traditional order had already begun to shift as merchants and traders in cities gained more power and wealth. One result of the Great Mortality in Europe was to speed up the pace of these changes.

Since there were fewer servants and skilled workers because so many people had died, those who were still alive began to demand higher wages—and better treatment too. They could always find another job, after all. This meant peasants were able to earn more, sometimes enough to purchase land for the first time. Some families became prosperous enough to pass on farms to their children, improving their standard of living. On the other hand, after the Great Mortality, rich landowners were often the losers. Since they had to pay workers more, they had to sell off parts of their estates or rent more of their land.

Of course, those in power wanted to return to how things had been, when they had more control and wealth. In the aftermath of the Great Mortality in England, wealthy leaders made efforts to impose new taxes and set limits on what peasants and skilled workers (artisans) such as bakers, carpenters, cobblers, tailors, and butchers could be paid for their services or goods. The first popular rebellion in England took place in 1381, as a protest against new tax collection officials and their harsh methods. The unrest didn't last long, and wasn't entirely successful, but it did end some kinds of taxation.

But in the uncertainty and unrest that followed the Great Mortality, one thing didn't change entirely: Plague was here to stay.

Adapting to Life with Plague

The Great Mortality may have ended, but plague didn't actually disappear. The disease returned to different parts of Europe, Asia, and Africa regularly over the next three hundred years—often in short, ferocious spurts lasting a year or two.

No wonder the word *plague* has seeped into our language. For instance, we "avoid something like the plague." As a verb, *plague* means to be bothered or harassed,

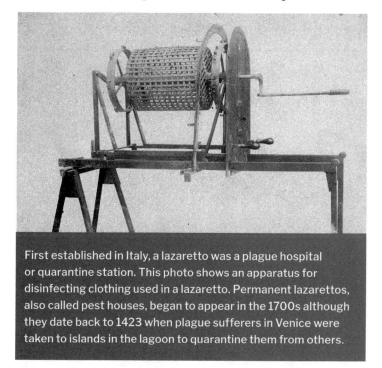

First established in Italy, a lazaretto was a plague hospital or quarantine station. This photo shows an apparatus for disinfecting clothing used in a lazaretto. Permanent lazarettos, also called pest houses, began to appear in the 1700s although they date back to 1423 when plague sufferers in Venice were taken to islands in the lagoon to quarantine them from others.

such as "to be plagued by mosquitoes." Over the centuries, people have most definitely been "plagued" by plague!

We know that during the Great Mortality, people died from both bubonic and pneumonic plague. After the mid-1300s, bubonic plague seems to have been the main form of the disease. The Great Plague of 1665 was the last major epidemic to hit London. It killed an estimated 100,000 people. Although they were not as

A seventeenth-century artist's depiction of a protective outfit worn by a plague doctor.

horrific as the Great Mortality, these waves of plague continued to cost lives and impact society.

Medicine still hadn't found a cause or a treatment for plague, but physicians continued to study the human body and how it functioned. During the Great Mortality, many priests and doctors had perished serving others. There was a need for more educated people in society. Some universities had been around for centuries, and after the Great Mortality, many more were established in Europe. New programs in medicine appeared as rivals to existing famous medical schools in Paris, Montpellier, Bologna, and Salerno. All this helped accelerate discoveries in medicine and science.

During the late 1300s and throughout the 1400s, more and more communities established systems, policies, and public health agencies to respond to the disease. This enabled them to take action whenever it appeared. English towns were some of the last to put public health in place, and some didn't act until the late 1500s.

The End of the Second Pandemic in Europe

The last major outbreak of plague in western Europe was the Great Plague of Marseille in 1720 to 1722 in France, which killed 100,000 people over two years across southern France. Still, plague outbreaks continued for another century in Europe.

Plague's Second Pandemic finally came to an end. But the shadow of this deadly disease still loomed. The threat never completely went away.

As we detectives already know, plague will always be with us. And it wasn't long before the disease reared its head again, this time in Asia.

CHAPTER 8
The Plague Fighter

Dr. Wu Lien-teh.

D r. Wu Lien-teh was born in Malaysia to Chinese parents in 1879. This unlikely hero of public health came of age at a critical moment in the history of the disease.

After long decades in western Europe when plague

outbreaks had become rare, plague had begun to reemerge in the 1850s in China. Although the boundaries between the Second Pandemic and the Third are somewhat blurred, most historians mark this as the start of the Third Pandemic.

However, despite advances in medicine, scientists were still in the dark about this mysterious disease. No effective cure was on the horizon. (Sulfonamide was first used to treat plague in 1938. Since 1946, the preferred course of treatment is the antibiotic streptomycin.) No one had yet identified the bacterium responsible for plague. No one fully recognized the role of rats and fleas. No one knew exactly how people got infected.

At the same time, cities were getting larger and more crowded. Shipping connected ports around the globe. Unlike the fourteenth century, many people now used some form of public transportation every day—trains, buses, and streetcars. The risks of a devastating plague outbreak were greater than ever.

An Almost Forgotten Hero

Wu Lien-teh didn't come from a rich family. But he was bright, ambitious, and eager to learn. During his childhood, Malaysia was under the control of Great Britain, so he spoke English at school. "The fees were low, varying from six to twelve dollars a year, so that even the poorest children could take advantage of it," he recalled.

Dr. Wu's path was unusual for a Chinese doctor at the time. He won a Queen's Scholarship to attend Cambridge University in England. There, he studied science and medicine with a special interest in **bacteriology**, the study of bacteria. Money was tight; he kept applying for scholarships just "to keep my head above water," he said.

In 1902, Wu Lien-teh became the first Chinese person to graduate in medicine from Cambridge. Dr. Wu went on to do advanced research fellowships in England and France. He was fascinated by the ways that medicine could help prevent deaths from epidemics, so he focused on infectious diseases such as malaria and tuberculosis.

Dr. Wu also studied at the Pasteur Institute in Paris, founded in 1888 by Dr. Louis Pasteur, who helped prove that diseases are caused by germs. For centuries, people didn't know that microorganisms like bacteria and viruses can cause infections because they had no way to see them. Then, in 1656, a German scholar named Athanasius Kircher became one of the first to observe microbes through a microscope. When he found what he called "little worms" in the blood of plague victims, Kircher proposed that there must be some kind of tiny living organism that was making people sick. It wasn't until stronger microscopes were developed in the 1870s, however, that scientists had the tools to really develop the germ theory.

Coincidentally, two researchers who, like Dr. Wu, trained at the Pasteur Institute, were able to identify the bacteria that causes plague.

PUTTING ALL THE PIECES TOGETHER

I. Discovering the Cause of Plague

When plague broke out again in the late nineteenth century, scientists grew even more determined to find the cause. One researcher in the chase was Swiss/French biologist Alexandre Yersin. Dr. Yersin loved adventure and travel. After studying at the Pasteur Institute in Paris, he became a doctor on merchant ships in Asia.

A plague outbreak in 1894 in Hong Kong sent him back to the lab. He lived in a straw hut on the grounds of a Hong Kong hospital and devoted himself to researching plague. In June of 1894, Dr. Yersin isolated the plague bacterium. He described it as "small stocky spindles with rounded ends" and named it *Pasteurella pestis* for his mentor, Louis Pasteur. It was later renamed *Yersinia pestis* in his honor. (Dr. Kitasato Shibasaburō of Japan was also in Hong Kong to do research. He identified plague bacteria a few days before Dr. Yersin. But since Dr. Yersin published his results first and explained more clearly what he'd found, he received the credit.)

Dr. Yersin identified the same bacteria in rodents, which suggested a possible link. However, scientists still weren't sure how it was transmitted from rats to humans. A few years after Dr. Yersin's discovery, another scientist from the Pasteur Institute figured it out, thanks to an ingenious experiment—and with the help of a cat.

II. Thanks to a Cat: Dr. Simond's Ingenious Experiment

Dr. Paul-Louis Simond followed in Dr. Yersin's footsteps and was doing plague research in India and Karachi (now the largest city in Pakistan) in 1897 and 1898. There was a large plague outbreak there at the time,

Putting All the Pieces Together

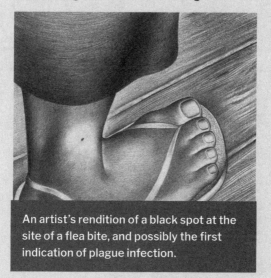

An artist's rendition of a black spot at the site of a flea bite, and possibly the first indication of plague infection.

and Dr. Simond noticed that plague patients sometimes had a visible small blister on their skin. He found that the blister contained fluid and plague bacilli. There was something else too: The little blister made him think of an insect bite.

Dr. Simond also discovered that rats could get plague if they were pricked with a contaminated needle. That led him to wonder: Could a biting insect like a flea play a part in how the disease spread—from rat to rat, and rat to human?

The Deadliest Diseases Then and Now

While staying at a hotel in Karachi in 1898, Dr. Simond designed an experiment to find out. He caught a plague-infected rat and placed it in a large glass container with sand on the bottom to absorb urine. He wanted to know if fleas could get plague and give it to another creature. To test his idea, he introduced some new, healthy fleas into the experiment.

"'I took advantage of the generosity of a cat I found stalking the hotel premises, borrowing some fleas from it,'" Dr. Simond said. He put the fleas from the healthy cat in the same container as the sick rat.

Then, Dr. Simond introduced another rat. He was careful to make sure it touched nothing. He suspended the rat in a wire cage so the newcomer had no contact with the plague rat or the container itself.

What do you think happened?

Within a day, the first rat died. Five days later, the new rat began to move slowly. "'By the evening of the sixth day it was dead. An autopsy of this one (previously uninfected rat) revealed buboes...'" said

Dr. Simond. He had shown that the new rat got bubonic plague from fleas.

At first, other scientists were skeptical. Eventually, the medical world recognized he was right: Fleas are a vector for plague.

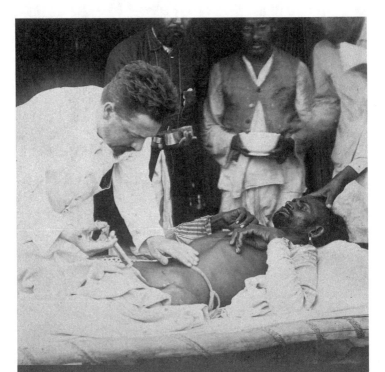

Dr. Paul-Louis Simond injecting a new (though unsuccessful) plague serum treatment in June 1898 in what is now Karachi, Pakistan. Since the 1940s, plague has been treated with the antibiotic streptomycin, which has also been used to treat tuberculosis.

Death in Winter

While scientists like Dr. Yersin and Dr. Simond were piecing together the basics of how plague works, Dr. Wu Lien-teh was finishing his college career. He returned to Malaysia to practice medicine. In 1908, he took a job training army doctors in Tianjin, a city in northeast China.

That's where Dr. Wu was in the fall of 1910, when plague broke out in Harbin, a city in Manchuria, a region in northeast China. Dr. Wu was asked to help out. Although he was only thirty-one, Dr. Wu became the "commander in chief" of a desperate effort to stop a ferocious and deadly outbreak.

Dr. Wu faced serious challenges. Russia and Japan controlled parts of the area along with China. Dr. Wu would have to find a way to work with officials of several countries, who were all nervous that plague might race across their borders.

Most of all, he would have to stop the plague epidemic and save lives.

Different and Dangerous

Rats, of course, are key to the story of the Great Mortality. And in the late 1800s, a strain of rat-borne plague germ (*Y. pestis* biovar orientalis) had spread around the world, hitting port cities in India and China very hard.

But this outbreak in 1910 in Manchuria was different. First, it was caused by hunters, who caught the disease by interacting with marmots infected with plague. Second, the Harbin epidemic wasn't bubonic plague. Dr. Wu immediately suspected people were dying from primary pneumonic plague, the contagious, lethal form of the disease, which kills 100 percent of its victims if not treated.

A severe outbreak of pneumonic plague hadn't been seen for centuries. No one alive had experience in combating this fierce enemy. It would be up to Dr. Wu to stop it.

Dr. Wu set off within two days of being asked to help. He remembered that "up to then very little had been known of the infection and much initiative as well as courage was required for its prevention and treatment."

The young physician was walking into the unknown. It must have been like walking into the Great Mortality.

Listen to the Marmots

For centuries, herders and local people in rural areas had eaten tarbagan marmots (*Marmota sibirica*), a large burrowing rodent found in China, Mongolia, Manchuria, and Russia. We know the roots of the Great Mortality probably can be traced to the disease passing from marmots to humans. And even today, marmots infected with plague can still pose problems if they are not handled safely.

In the early 1900s, marmots were trapped for their fur, which, because of new dyes, could be passed off as the more valuable pelts of sable or mink. This caused such a rush on marmot hunting that many inexperienced

Marmots serve as natural reservoirs for plague bacteria in nature. Hunters in Manchuria who came in contact with plague-infected marmots contracted the disease, leading to a severe outbreak of human plague in 1910–1911.

trappers flocked to the region eager to hunt and make money. However, these newcomers didn't know how to tell a healthy animal from a plague-infected one.

Healthy marmots can be found in the open fields rather than huddled in their burrows. Sick marmots are also unsteady and slow. Another hint to an animal's health is the sound they make. In a 1911 speech, Dr. Wu noted that "the healthy marmot basking, as it loves to do, in the warm sunshine, utters a cry resembling the sound 'Pu p'a, pu p'a.'"

This, he explained, sounds a bit like a Chinese phrase meaning "don't be afraid," or "no harm." He went on to say that a sick marmot is silent. So "when the marmot isn't crying, 'no harm, no harm,' there is a very real harm indeed!"

Experienced local hunters knew that it was important to stay away from plague-infected marmots. But the new hunters apparently didn't listen to their warnings. In October of 1910, the first reports of men falling ill with headaches and fever appeared. Some victims spit up blood and died—the telltale signs of contagious pneumonic plague.

The hunters often gathered together in market towns and lived in close quarters in poorly ventilated huts. The living conditions were harsh. The huts were like simple dormitories with berths. The men had to cook, eat, and sleep in a single room. To make things worse, the frigid weather meant that windows were kept closed. These conditions made it easy for plague to spread rapidly.

Also, like the coronavirus, plague didn't stay in one place. As the itinerant hunters returned home to celebrate Chinese New Year on January 30, 1911, the plague traveled along with them—by railway and road, and even by sea.

A dangerous outbreak had begun.

Plague Fighter at Work

Dr. Wu arrived in plague-infected Harbin on a bitterly cold December day. The young doctor faced enormous challenges. The scene was chaotic. Many frightened and panicked residents of the city had fled. There were bodies lying in the streets. Others corpses were piled up, impossible to bury in the frozen ground. One of Dr. Wu's first acts was to seek the government's permission

During the outbreak in Harbin, Dr. Wu Lien-teh introduced techniques still in use by epidemiologists today. Note the personal protective equipment (PPE) being worn by the health care worker on the right.

to cremate three thousand plague victims, whose bodies posed a public health risk.

Although autopsies weren't normally performed in China at this time, Dr. Wu was able to get approval to conduct one. The results confirmed his suspicion: He was up against pneumonic plague. And he was pretty much on his own to figure out what to do.

Fortunately, Dr. Wu was up to the task.

Dr. Wu knew pneumonic plague was contagious and lethal. He wasn't about to take chances. He immediately put in place practices such as wearing masks, isolating contacts, hospitalizing victims, and disinfecting the homes of patients. Today, we know face masks and other kinds of **personal protective equipment (PPE)** help prevent people from transmitting or contracting some infectious diseases.

These are the best tools of public health practices. But not everyone in Harbin accepted Dr. Wu's advice. At the Russian plague hospital, none of the health care workers wore masks; some later died. Dr. Wu encountered the same resistance to his recommendations when a well-known French doctor named Gerard Mesny arrived.

Dr. Mesny was more familiar with bubonic plague and underestimated the extreme danger of pneumonic plague. He also underestimated Dr. Wu. Dr. Mesny

Dr. Wu Lien-teh used multilayered gauze face masks as well as full protective body suits during the pneumonic plague outbreak in 1910–1911.

resented being told what to do by the young Chinese physician. And so he refused to wear a mask.

He caught plague and died.

Following this tragedy, health care workers in Harbin willingly followed Dr. Wu's methods. Dr. Wu also convinced local officials to suspend train travel to help keep the disease from spreading to other places. He launched efforts to inspect houses to find new cases and worked to isolate the sick and their contacts.

Dr. Wu was racing against time. Remember, without antibiotics, which weren't yet available, the mortality rate for pneumonic plague is 100 percent.

Thanks to his use of sound public health practices, Dr. Wu's actions helped stop the outbreak and saved many lives. By March 31, 1911, infections had stopped. This outbreak could have spread to several countries with tragic results. In recognition of his achievement in controlling the epidemic, Dr. Wu was nominated for the Nobel Prize in Medicine in 1935. He was the first Chinese doctor to receive a Nobel nomination.

Dr. Wu had a brilliant career. He became a hero in the international medical community. During the 2020 coronavirus pandemic, scientists paid tribute to the example he set in putting in place the tools of controlling highly contagious diseases: face masks, personal protective equipment, isolation, and contact tracing.

Dr. Wu's friends called him Tuck. Even when he became famous, he remained modest and dedicated to his profession. He died in 1960 at the age of eighty-one.

The Toll of the Third Pandemic

The late 1800s brought new knowledge of plague, thanks to the discovery of plague bacteria in 1894 in Hong Kong during an outbreak there. Dr. Wu's public health work during the 1910–1911 plague outbreak in China helped bring international attention to how using personal protective equipment and tracing contacts could aid in controlling outbreaks.

But since effective antibiotic treatments weren't available until the 1930s, the Third Pandemic still had a devastating impact around the world, especially in India. According to the World Health Organization, "The third pandemic began in Canton and Hong Kong in 1894 and spread rapidly throughout the world, by rats aboard the swifter steamships that replaced slow-moving sailing vessels in merchant fleets. Within 10 years (1894–1903) plague entered 77 ports on five continents. Plague became widespread in a number of countries. In India, there were over 6 million deaths from 1898 to 1908."

Plague also came to San Francisco in the early years of the twentieth century, bringing with it elements of racial and ethnic prejudice against the city's Chinese community, echoing what we saw in medieval Europe, when people blamed Jews for the Great Mortality.

The first cases in San Francisco appeared in 1900 in Chinatown, a thriving business and cultural area of the city. But anti-Chinese sentiments were strong. There were false claims that people of European descent couldn't catch the disease. Residents of Chinatown were subjected to prejudice, intimidation, house-to-house searches, and campaigns to disinfect rooms and houses. Disinfecting was tried first since some people still weren't aware of or willing to accept the findings linking plague to rats and fleas.

There was also resistance to anti-plague public health measures by some leaders, who didn't want to admit the disease had come to the city because it would be bad for business. The outbreak lasted until February of 1904. There were about 126 cases and 122 deaths. In 1907, following the San Francisco earthquake and fire of 1906, cases of plague were reported. However, this time, officials applied the latest scientific information and launched a rat-catching campaign.

Fortunately, as the twentieth century progressed, plague deaths continued to decrease, thanks to more knowledge about the disease and newly available treatments. Port cities were hit hard in the Third Pandemic. But new knowledge linking rats and fleas to the disease led to more efforts to control rat populations in maritime ports and on ships. Deaths in 1907 were more than a million, but dropped to 22,000 in 1939–1948 and 4,600 in 1949–1953.

The world's long nightmare with plague was ending.

But what about the future? Would plague strike again?

CHAPTER 9
Will Plague Strike Again?

I t's easy to think of plague as a disease from a time long past. But as we've seen, that's not the case. The fear of plague runs deep and still has a grip on people's imaginations. Even single cases are international news. In July of 2020, after a herdsman in Mongolia contracted bubonic plague from a marmot, local officials put restrictions on hunting, eating, or transporting infected animals for the rest of the year.

When reports like these occur, it's natural to wonder whether plague is still a danger today. Could plague strike again? When you read about cases of plague breakout out in China, Mongolia, or even the United States, should you worry?

The simple answer is no. The ability of plague to

spread is far less than it was in the past. In part, that's because we can treat it with antibiotics, which kill the bacteria. We can track cases quickly. Human hygiene, housing standards, and nutrition have also improved tremendously. As a result, fewer people in the world live in close contact with rats, lice, and fleas.

Nevertheless, plague is still deadly if left untreated. So we can't completely forget about plague. It's still one of three infectious diseases that countries must report to the World Health Organization (WHO) so that cases can be monitored and tracked. (As of this writing, cholera and yellow fever also must be reported.)

WHO has reported that between 2010 and 2015 there were 3,248 cases of plague around the world, with 584 deaths. However, in 2017, a serious plague epidemic broke out in Madagascar, where plague persists in animal populations. The WHO reported that from August to November of 2017, there were more than 2,400 cases and 209 deaths from plague. WHO delivered emergency funds and antibiotics, and trained more than 4,000 people to trace the contacts of infected people to help keep the disease from spreading.

In addition to the need to respond to sporadic outbreaks, governments around the world keep watch on plague for another reason. Strains of plague that resist antibiotics could be used as weapons during a war. Should this ever happen, and we hope it never will, quarantine would be the only way to control the disease.

Our best defense is to work for peace, invest in science, and make sure plague becomes something just to read about in books. And remember, always be cautious around wild creatures or any animal that looks sick or infected.

Americans wore masks during the 1918 influenza pandemic. Left: a streetcar conductor in Seattle reminds passengers that masks are required. Right: A street sweeper in New York. To persuade people to wear masks, the New York Health Board used the slogan "Better be ridiculous than dead."

Part Three

GLOBAL DISASTER: THE 1918 INFLUENZA PANDEMIC

MASK WORN TO CHECK INFLUENZA SPREAD.

The admonition of the New York Health Board to wear masks to check the spread of the influenza epidemic has been heeded: "Better be ridiculous than dead", is the view of one official.

A 1918 INFLUENZA FAMILY TRAGEDY

Some years ago, librarian Karen Drevo invited me to a literature festival in Nebraska. I never forgot hearing the heartbreaking family story she told me, and she has graciously shared it here.

My grandmother, Mary Ethel Rodaway Wyatt, and her first cousin, Florence Stutt Crandell, grew up together and were best friends. They both got married in 1917 and had babies in 1918. Grandma told me that during the fall of 1918, schools and churches were closed in Otoe County, Nebraska, and farmers such as my grandparents isolated themselves on their farms. Grandpa was the only one who would go to town and he would only go when it was absolutely necessary.

Shortly after Florence gave birth, she invited my grandparents and their baby daughter to come to Sunday dinner to meet Florence's new baby. After months of isolating themselves, my grandparents decided there would be no harm in going to visit Florence and her husband and the new baby on their nearby farm. Afterward, at about 4:00 p.m., my grandparents went home to do the chores.

Early the next morning, they received a call from Florence's husband to say that after they left, Florence and the new baby took ill, and within hours, both had died of influenza.

Grandma and Grandpa were sure they and their baby daughter would get the influenza since they had been in close contact with Florence and the baby for hours. But my grandparents, their baby, and Florence's husband never contracted the influenza. Grandma told me that that strain of influenza was especially hard on young women who had just given birth and their babies.

Florence was buried with her baby in her arms. Grandma never got over the shock and grieved the rest of her life for Florence.

—Karen Drevo

CHAPTER 10

The Deadliest Flu Outbreak in History

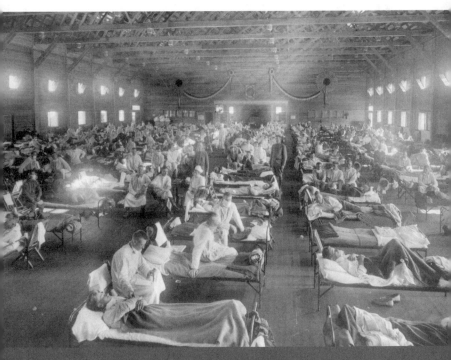

An emergency influenza hospital at Camp Funston, a large army training camp near Fort Riley, Kansas, where the global influenza pandemic reared its head in March of 1918.

On March 11, 1918, a soldier at Fort Riley, Kansas, went to the camp hospital. He complained of typical flu symptoms: a fever, sore throat, a headache. There was nothing unusual about that.

However, within a week, five hundred more soldiers became sick. And the outcome *was* unusual: Forty-eight young, healthy soldiers died that spring.

Flu usually strikes older people hardest. What was going on?

Severe cases of flu had been popping up elsewhere in Kansas around this time. Reports of bad flu appeared in other parts of the world too. Where did this deadly influenza begin? Researchers are still not sure—and may never know the answer. What they do know is that by the summer of 1918 this deadly influenza was affecting people everywhere, becoming an explosive pandemic.

Scientists think it started in birds, probably wild waterfowl, a natural reservoir of the virus. They also know the 1918 virus was what's categorized as an influenza virus A subtype H1N1 strain that has emerged again in other outbreaks, including the "swine flu" in 2009–2010. (More on influenza viruses and vaccines later.)

One thing is certain. Although it's still sometimes called the **Spanish flu**, this devastating flu didn't start in Spain. So how did it get this nickname? Well, Spain was a neutral country during World War I, which meant there was no wartime censorship. Governments in other countries were reluctant to report the impact of the flu on troops for fear the news might impact their war efforts. Since the flu seemed to be hitting Spain hard, simply because more cases were openly reported there in newspapers, it picked up that nickname.

Flu, of course, is an abbreviation of the word *influenza*, which comes from the Italian word meaning "influence," which is from the medieval Latin word *influentia*. It came into use around 1500, and may originally have meant coming under the influence of the stars, or coming under the influence of the cold. After an outbreak in Italy in 1743, *influenza* became the term commonly used to describe the flu. Influenza is caused by viruses, which are different from bacteria in that they are not considered to be alive.

The word *virus* means "poison" in Latin. Although by 1918, scientists had not yet identified or isolated any viruses in the lab, they had made progress in understanding bacteria. And now they knew other things besides bacteria caused diseases. For example, when they removed all the bacteria from an infected tissue sample, the infection was still present. That meant, using the process of elimination, there must be another cause for some diseases, including influenza. Scientists were finally able to look at viruses in the 1930s, through powerful electron microscopes that use beams of electrons to magnify very small objects.

Conditions for a Global Disaster

The first flu cases broke out during the spring of 1918. World War I, which lasted from July 28, 1914, until November 11, 1918, was winding down. (The war ended on the eleventh hour of the eleventh day of the eleventh month. In the United States, November 11 is a national holiday, Veterans Day.)

Conditions were ripe for the rapid spread of the disease. Soldiers were still living together in close quarters, which ignited the spread. Troops were still in training and on battlefields. The end of the war meant millions of soldiers traveling home, spreading the virus far and wide. People living and working in close quarters were especially vulnerable.

For example, in England, where civilians had suffered four years of wartime food shortages and food rations during the war, the disease hit hard, felling coal miners and factory workers. Like other infectious diseases, large gatherings, such as people attending London theaters and music halls, led to more infections.

In the United States, both troop movements and autumn victory parades following the end of the war in November led to spikes of infection. And it wasn't just soldiers. The flu also struck miners and people living in crowded cities across the globe, causing death tolls not seen since the Great Mortality. The pandemic reached Guam, Africa, South America, the Pacific Islands, China, and India, where it killed millions.

Warnings Were Ignored

The 1918 influenza pandemic had three waves: during the spring of 1918, the devastating upsurge in the fall of 1918, and finally a third wave in the spring of 1919.

Without any available treatment, experts relied on the strategies used successfully by Dr. Wu Lien-teh in the Manchuria plague epidemic just a few years before. But isolation, quarantining, use of masks, and restrictions on large public gatherings didn't always happen.

In some cases, officials ignored warnings with devastating results. A parade in Philadelphia had been planned to sell war bonds to help pay for the war effort. Despite concerns about crowds, officials didn't cancel the event. The Liberty Loan Parade took place on September 28, 1918.

About 200,000 people packed the sidewalks to

Crowds packed the Liberty Loan Parade in Philadelphia in September of 1918. As a result, 12,000 people died from influenza.

cheer on marching bands, Scouts, and soldiers, sailors, and marines. Two days later, influenza was racing through the city. Hospitals filled to capacity. The daily death toll continued to explode.

It's estimated that within a week, 45,000 people got sick. In the end, 12,000 died. The parade remains a heartbreaking lesson in the danger of gathering in large crowds when an infectious disease is on the loose.

One-Third of the World

While during its three pandemics in recorded history, plague has killed many hundreds of millions, the Centers for Disease Control and Prevention (CDC) ranks the 1918 influenza pandemic as the deadliest event in recent time. It sickened more than 500 million people—about one-third of the world's population at the time. Within one year, flu took the lives of up to 50 million people, 675,000 of them in the United States alone. More people died of the virus than World War I, and it was particularly deadly for children under five and for young, healthy adults.

The Deadliest Diseases Then and Now

As memories and survivors of this pandemic pass into history, it's important to remember the suffering and heartbreak it caused to individuals and families around the world. In 2018, the CDC compiled first-person survivor accounts. You can read their stories here: https://www.cdc.gov/publications/panflu/stories /survived.html.

Scientists understand that new influenza viruses can emerge again at any time. The potential for future pandemics is real. In our connected world, infectious diseases can move faster than ever. The tools of epidemiology: wearing face masks, isolating, hand washing, and physical distancing will continue to be part of our lives.

MORE ON INFLUENZA OUTBREAKS AND VACCINES

Scientists still study the 1918 flu pandemic, and there's a good reason. Since 1918, all subsequent influenza A pandemics and seasonal epidemics have been caused by descendants of the 1918 virus. This includes flu pandemics in 1957, 1968, and 2009.

There are four different kinds of influenza viruses, which scientists have labeled A, B, C, and D. Only the A and B kinds are dangerous to people, with virus A being the one that causes deadly pandemics. Influenza type A viruses are also categorized into subtypes (that's why you see H and N and different numbers, like H1N1).

Each year, more than one subtype of the A virus circulates at the same time as the B virus. The colder months are known as the flu season, because that's when most people get sick from the disease. Those who create vaccines play a guessing game each year, trying to determine both the number of dosages needed and the combination of viruses likely to reoccur.

A flu vaccine causes **antibodies** to develop in our body about two weeks later. Antibodies help protect against infection with the viruses—but only the ones used to make the vaccine. Each year, researchers create the seasonal flu vaccine based on guesses as to which viruses will be most prevalent in the coming season. Most flu vaccines in the United States protect against four different flu viruses.

In 2009, a strain of flu known as the **(H1N1)pdm09 virus** appeared. It was called the swine flu because the virus was also found in pig populations.

It was quite different from other H1N1 viruses at this time. Very few young people seemed to have any existing immunity, although nearly a third of people age sixty or older did. That probably meant that sometime in their lives, older people had been exposed to a similar virus.

But the seasonal flu vaccine that year simply didn't offer protection against this new virus. The CDC estimates that from April 2009 until April 2010, there were more than 60 million cases of this flu, resulting in nearly 275,000 Americans being hospitalized and 12,469 deaths. Around the world, as many as 500,000 people died, 80 percent of them younger than age sixty-five. (Normally, most deaths from flu occur in the elderly.) WHO declared an end to the global 2009 H1N1 influenza pandemic in August 2010, but (H1N1)pdm09 virus continues to circulate each flu season.

The CDC recommends that everyone six months and older get a vaccine, or flu shot, by the end of October of each year. Flu shots help protect ourselves, and also those around us who may be more vulnerable or have other diseases.

A highly magnified image of the features of an *Anopheles dirus* mosquito's antennae. Malaria is caused by a parasite and spread through a vector—the bite of an infected female *Anopheles* mosquito.

Malaria can be prevented by controlling mosquitoes, spraying indoors, and using mosquito nets for sleeping. According to WHO, there were more than 228 million cases of malaria in the world in 2018 and more than 400,000 deaths. Children under five, especially in Africa, are most at risk.

Acc.V   Spot Magn   Det   WD   E
30.0 kV 3.0   363x   SE   7.2   0

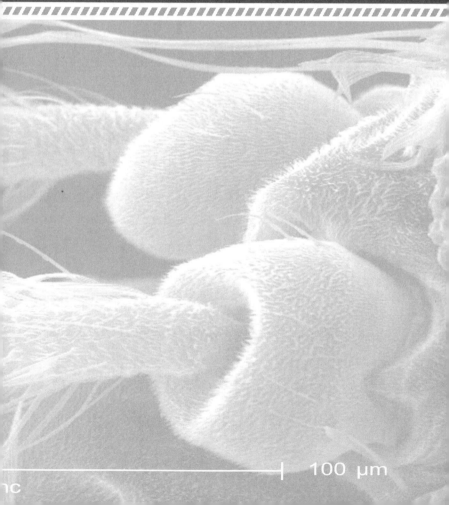

Part Four

OTHER DEADLY DISEASES THEN AND NOW

100 μm

CHAPTER 11

Diseases Are Here to Stay

The shadow of the Great Mortality haunts our history and our language. But plague and the 1918 influenza pandemic are not the only infectious diseases that have "plagued" people throughout time. This section chronicles a few others. Some have been around for centuries. Others, like the coronavirus pandemic that began in late 2019, are brand-new.

Despite the advances of modern medicine, pandemics loom in humanity's future as well. Some experts expect disease outbreaks will become more frequent as climate change erodes ecosystems and brings human populations and wildlife into closer contact.

Vaccines have helped lessen the suffering and loss of life brought on by infectious diseases. Still, many continue to pose problems for global health, especially for vulnerable communities and children.

Cholera

Plague was not the only disease that spread across the world in waves. Epidemics of cholera were frequent in the 1800s. Cholera is caused by a bacterium that lives naturally in salty water in the lower Ganges River region between modern-day India and Bangladesh.

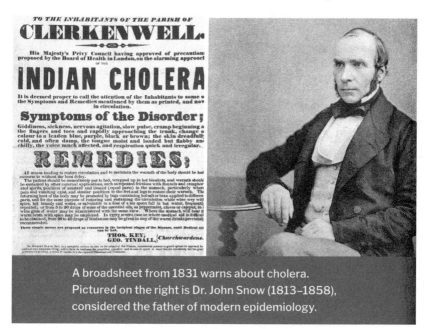

A broadsheet from 1831 warns about cholera.
Pictured on the right is Dr. John Snow (1813–1858),
considered the father of modern epidemiology.

Unlike the plague and the flu, the bacteria that causes cholera doesn't live within an animal or insect host. It is often found in water. During the 1800s and 1900s, seven waves of the disease occurred.

In the 1800s, the valiant efforts of Dr. John Snow in England helped change the way people understood diseases and how to prevent them in order to protect public health.

Little was known about cholera, which causes severe vomiting, diarrhea, and death. Most doctors at the time were convinced it was caused by—you guessed it—miasma: polluted, smelly air.

Dr. Snow believed cholera was caused by contaminated water, *not* by miasma. He felt sure there must be some sort of poison in the water. Whatever it was, it was too small for him to see through his microscope.

In 1854, when cholera broke out on Broad Street in London, Dr. Snow wanted to prove that those falling sick had drunk water from one central well on Broad Street, which was used for drinking water.

He made a map of the neighborhood, like modern epidemiologists do now. He was able to link those who got sick to the Broad Street pump. On September 8, 1854, John convinced local officials to remove the handle of the pump to protect the community. His actions saved many lives.

Several months later, the reason for the outbreak was discovered. A leak was found underground between the bricks of the well and the cesspit of 40 Broad Street, a nearby house. The Lewis family lived there, and when five-month-old Frances Lewis got sick, her mother rinsed her diapers out in the cesspit. The cholera bacteria from her feces was seeping into the well water and infecting many of those who drank it.

Dr. Snow is often called the father of modern public health.

Cholera is caused by the bacterium *Vibrio cholerae*. *V. cholerae* enters the body when someone drinks water or eats undercooked food that contains the bacterium.

The bacterium can also be spread by flies that land on the feces of infected persons and carry the bacterium to other people's clothing and blankets. Outbreaks are more likely to occur when water or food sources are contaminated with human feces containing the bacteria. Poor sanitation; the lack of safe, clean drinking water; poverty; and the disruption of water supplies by natural disaster or conflicts can lead to cholera outbreaks.

Although cholera can be prevented with a vaccine and can be treated with antibiotics, it still affects more than four million people in the world each year.

Smallpox Success!

We know that plague won't ever completely go away. In fact, there is only one deadly disease that has ever been eradicated: smallpox. The elimination of smallpox is one of humanity's most remarkable accomplishments. It came about thanks to a decades-long global effort led by WHO. It's a reminder of what can be accomplished when everyone pulls together for the good of all.

Smallpox may date back thousands of years. It's caused by the **variola virus**, which produced a rash and blisters on patients' bodies. This contagious disease caused death in about 30 percent of victims. The number of deaths is staggering—some experts believe that in the twentieth century alone, smallpox killed 300 million people all over the world. Like plague, it was feared for hundreds of years.

Smallpox has a unique place in history. In 1796, Edward Jenner moved the science of vaccination forward when he found a safe way to protect people from smallpox by inoculating them with cowpox, a less serious disease. Before that, the practice copied from Asia was to inoculate people with bits of infectious scab taken from other people's smallpox sores, in the hope that would cause a mild infection. Smallpox is also the only infectious disease to be eliminated worldwide by the use of a vaccine.

In 1959, WHO announced a goal of eradicating smallpox everywhere. At first, however, there simply weren't enough resources or money to make it a success. Smallpox continued to claim lives in South America, Africa, and Asia.

People didn't give up. In 1967, the international health community decided to intensify its efforts. New vaccination campaigns and case tracking took place. Success came slowly, but in 1971 smallpox had been eliminated from South America. In 1975, a three-year-old girl in Bangladesh became the last person to naturally get *Variola major*, the more severe form of the disease. She was isolated until she recovered to prevent it from spreading. About two years later, Ali Maow Maalin in Somalia became the last person on earth to acquire *Variola minor* naturally.

According to the CDC, "Almost two centuries after Jenner published his hope that vaccination could annihilate smallpox, on May 8, 1980, the 33rd World Health Assembly officially declared the world free of this disease. Eradication of smallpox is considered the biggest achievement in international public health."

ALI MAOW MAALIN: SMALLPOX SURVIVOR AND POLIO FIGHTER

Ali Maow Maalin, the last person to get naturally occurring smallpox (*Variola minor*, the milder form of the disease), dedicated his life to protecting children from polio.

The Deadliest Diseases Then and Now

In 1977, Ali Maow Maalin (1954–2013) was a hospital cook near Mogadishu in Somalia when he became the last person in the world to become naturally infected with smallpox. He got the disease driving two young children to get medical care.

Ali, who had feared getting vaccinated, later used his experience to help others. He began working on a campaign to vaccinate children in Somalia from poliomyelitis. "'Now when I meet parents who refuse to give their children the polio vaccine, I tell them my story,' he once said. 'I tell them how important those vaccines are. I tell them not to do something foolish like me.'"

Ali became an inspiration to public health workers all over the world. He died of malaria in 2013, still working to protect the children of his country from polio.

Poliomyelitis

Ali Maow Maalin fought to vaccinate children against the devastating effects of poliomyelitis. This disease, caused by the poliovirus, destroys nerve cells in the spinal cord and can cause victims to be paralyzed, or without the ability to move.

In the first half of the twentieth century, polio became one of the most feared diseases. It affected tens

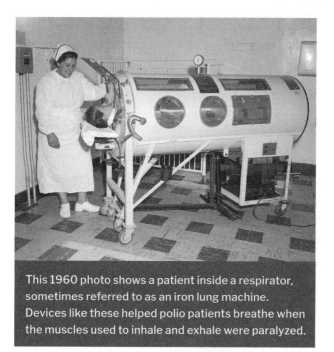

This 1960 photo shows a patient inside a respirator, sometimes referred to as an iron lung machine. Devices like these helped polio patients breathe when the muscles used to inhale and exhale were paralyzed.

of thousands each year, mostly young children. The virus sometimes struck adults as well. In 1921, Franklin D. Roosevelt contracted polio when he was thirty-nine. He went on to become president but suffered the effects of the disease for the rest of his life.

In the 1950s, Dr. Jonas Salk developed a successful vaccine for polio. A massive vaccination campaign was launched, and in 1954, hundreds of thousands of children across the United States took part in a large vaccine trial.

As a result of widespread vaccination, the United States has been free of polio cases since 1979. In 1988, WHO launched the Global Polio Eradication Initiative to eliminate it in other countries as well.

Although much progress has been made, the effort is still ongoing. The disease affects young children in some of the world's poorest nations. To see a map of current cases in the world, visit WHO at http://polio eradication.org/polio-today/polio-now/.

VACCINES SAVE LIVES

Vaccines help protect us against diseases. There are several different kinds of vaccines. For example, vaccines for the flu or polio use the whole virus that has been killed. Other vaccines, such as those for measles, chicken pox, and tuberculosis, work by using a live but weakened form of the virus. And still others work by using **antigens**, very small parts of the germ. In 2020, researchers developed vaccines against COVID-19 that use a new technology. Called **messenger RNA vaccines** (mRNA), these vaccines work by teaching our cells how to make a protein or piece of a protein to trigger an immune response in our bodies.

All vaccines have the same goal: To help our body's immune system go to work and produce antibodies to recognize and better fight off diseases. Vaccines are tested carefully for safety. Vaccines are important tools to help protect individuals and communities from serious diseases.

The Deadliest Diseases Then and Now

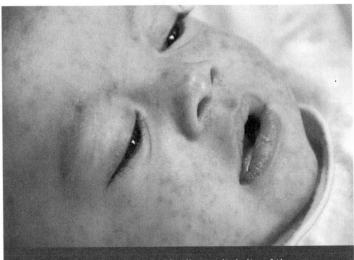

This photo shows a baby in Manila, capital city of the Philippines, who was hospitalized with measles in 2014. Measles is a serious and highly contagious disease that can lead to complications such as hearing loss, blindness, seizures, brain inflammation, and death. A safe and effective vaccine is available in the United States that protects against measles and two other diseases, mumps and rubella.

Tuberculosis

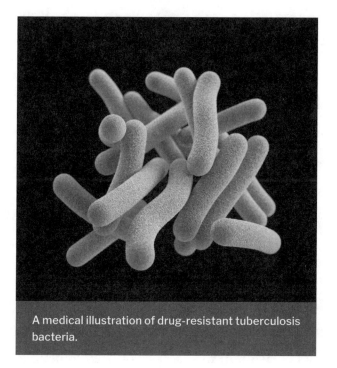

A medical illustration of drug-resistant tuberculosis bacteria.

Tuberculosis is a serious threat around the world. It's caused by a bacterium called *Mycobacterium tuberculosis*. Symptoms of the disease include coughing, chest pain, and feeling tired. Tuberculosis (TB) most often affects the lungs. Not everyone infected with TB gets sick, but if someone has TB, it's essential to get treated. The

CDC estimates that about thirteen million people in America carry the infection but are not actively ill.

Around the globe, ten million people get TB each year. About one and a half million die. Treatment with antibiotics is possible, although the process takes six months. However, some strains of TB don't respond to medicine and may take even longer to treat.

WHO also estimates that one-third of the population of the world has the TB bacteria in their bodies, though only a small portion will get sick. That's because in many people, the disease stays inactive. TB is rare in the United States, and a vaccine is not widely used. Some people may need to take a TB test for their job. They may work in food service or need to be tested to make sure they don't infect people in nursing homes or shelters.

HIV/AIDS: Devastating Global Epidemic of the Twentieth Century

HIV stands for human immunodeficiency virus. It mutated from a virus called simian immunodeficiency virus (SIV) that exists in primates like African green monkeys without causing them any disease. When other primates, such as chimpanzees, get infected, they get very sick and die. When the virus passed from sick chimpanzees into humans, and then from one human to another, it became known as the human immunodeficiency virus (HIV).

The HIV virus weakens a person's immune system, as it kills cells that can fight infection. There is no cure, but doctors

An HIV education and awareness poster from a health department in New Zealand in the 1990s.

now can control HIV. If untreated, the HIV virus can lead to acquired immunodeficiency syndrome (AIDS), the most serious stage of HIV infection. People don't die from AIDS itself, but from other diseases that their bodies are no longer capable of fighting, such as pneumonia.

The first case of AIDS emerged in the United States in 1981. Although HIV may have been in the United States since the 1970s, cases increased in the United States and in countries in Africa throughout the 1980s.

Africa remains the hardest-hit region in the world. According to WHO, seventy-six million people have been infected with HIV and thirty-three million have died. As of 2019, more than thirty-eight million people have HIV.

HIV is transmitted only in certain ways from a person who has HIV to another, through specific bodily fluids, including blood, breast milk, or when people participate in sexual activities without adequate protection. It is not transmitted through saliva, tears, feces, or the urine of a person with HIV.

Each year, on December 1, we celebrate World AIDS Day. This is a time when people around the world come together to show support for people living with HIV and to remember those who have died from AIDS-related illnesses. World AIDS Day was founded in 1988 by UNAIDS, the Joint United Nations Programme on HIV/AIDS, which is dedicated to leading global action against the disease, increasing awareness about the disease, and working to end discrimination against people with HIV/AIDS.

You can learn more about UNAIDS here: https://www.unaids.org/en.

Public health experts recommend that we wear face masks and keep physical distance of at least six feet from others outside our own household in order to prevent the spread of COVID-19.

Not sure how far six feet is? Try this: Get a tape measure and string. Then cut a piece of string six feet long. Next, practice placing your string between you and a family member, a chair, or a table. Before long, you'll be able to estimate safe physical distancing.

Practice Social Distancing

Stay 6 feet (2 arm's lengths) from other people.

Part Five

NOW:
THE TWENTY-FIRST CENTURY

nd Wear a Cloth Face Covering

"The coronavirus is bad in many ways, but the worst part of all is people get sick. It's also hard not being able to do all the fun things you could do before it happened. And when my mom was sick, it was super sad because I couldn't see her for two weeks while she quarantined all by herself."

— LILY, AGE 9, NEW YORK CITY, 2020

Be sure it covers your nose and mouth to help protect others. You could be infected and not have symptoms.

cdc.gov/coronavirus

CHAPTER 12
COVID-19

L et's return to Italy again. Only now it's 2020, more than 670 years after our imaginary Genoese merchant was felled by plague. In the books of the future, a man known only as Mattia, to protect his privacy, may appear as a footnote in the history of the 2020 coronavirus pandemic as Italy's Patient One, the first Italian to be officially diagnosed with the virus in his country. (Note to reader: Although Mattia was the first person to receive an official diagnosis, after our journey into plague history, you won't be surprised to hear that the story of how the virus got to Europe is still being revised as new information is found! In early 2021, just as this book was going to print, researchers announced they'd found evidence of the coronavirus taken from a child with measles in Milan, Italy, in early December 2019.)

A novel, or new, coronavirus appeared in Wuhan, China, sometime in the fall of 2019. It possibly passed from bats to humans. Other kinds of coronaviruses cause the common cold and much more serious diseases like SARS (Severe Acute Respiratory Syndrome) and MERS (Middle East Respiratory Syndrome).

On February 11, 2020, a WHO committee gave the virus its official name: severe acute respiratory syndrome coronavirus 2, or SARS-CoV-2. Most people simply called it the coronavirus. It's gotten nicknames too, such as "the corona," "COVID," or just "the virus."

The disease caused by SARS-CoV-2 was named coronavirus disease 2019, or COVID-19. The symptoms of COVID-19, which appear between two and fourteen days after exposure to the virus, include fever or chills, cough, shortness of breath, headaches, body aches, and sort throat, among others. Some people also lose their sense of taste and smell. Still others who test positive never feel very sick. But others suffer and may die. The disease attacks the lungs and also other parts of the body.

Mattia, a thirty-eight-year-old marathon runner, was the first Italian in his country to test positive for COVID-19: Patient One. He had not traveled out of Italy, but he developed flu-like symptoms and went to the hospital, where he fell gravely ill.

How did Mattia get the disease? Although Mattia is known as Patient One and was the first Italian to become sick, researchers believe that someone else, known as Patient Zero, brought the disease from elsewhere, just as in 1347, ships from the Black Sea region brought plague to Italy's shores.

In this case, Italy's Patient Zero was a German who had become infected with coronavirus. Patient Zero traveled to northern Italy around January 25, 2020. Mattia somehow came into contact with Patient Zero—and the disease began to spread in Italy, and kept spreading.

How did Patient Zero get it? Well, we now know the disease had spread out of Wuhan, China, in the bodies of unsuspecting business people, tourists, and travelers who then passed it on to others everywhere they went.

Researchers believe Patient Zero came in contact with someone who had been in China. And then, like so many others, that person passed the virus on without realizing it. In this way, the virus spread from person to person, reaching every country on earth.

As for Patient One, Mattia was lucky enough to survive. But little was known about the virus then. And without realizing it, Mattia likely infected many others, including his wife, who lived, and his father, who did not.

While much has changed since the Great Mortality and the 1918 influenza pandemic, Mattia's story reminds us: Diseases go where people go.

Although early in 2020, after some nations closed their borders and limited travel, it quickly became clear that the virus had already snuck in and was spreading throughout communities. We now know that when people speak, cough, sing, or yell, the virus spews into the air on tiny droplets, which can infect others.

While researchers continue to study how the disease may be transmitted through the air and ventilation

systems, we now know that practices like wearing a mask, keeping windows open, and maintaining a six-foot distance from others all help reduce the spread of COVID-19. Each of us must do our part to keep ourselves and our communities safe.

Unlike the 1918 flu pandemic, which was especially lethal to young healthy adults, COVID-19 has caused more deaths among older people. It has also been more deadly for people who already have poor health or underlying conditions like heart disease or diabetes. Communities of color that don't have equal health care or good access to health care in the United States have been hit especially hard. These include Black, Latinx, Native American, Asian, and Pacific Islander communities. Health care workers and people who serve the public and work in close contact with others, as well as those unable to do their jobs from home, have also been at greater risk.

On March 11, 2020, WHO declared the coronavirus outbreak a pandemic. At the time of the announcement, 118,000 people in 114 countries had tested positive for COVID-19, with 4,291 deaths. Six months later, on September 11, 2020, WHO reported 27,973,127 cases in 216 countries, with 905,426 deaths. In January 2021, as vaccination campaigns were still getting underway in some countries, WHO reported about 100 million cases worldwide and more than 2 million deaths. These numbers will be higher by the time you are reading this book.

Pandemics like the Great Mortality and the

coronavirus pandemic create other problems, such as job loss and hunger. In September of 2020, the United Nations World Food Program estimated that up to 260 million people in developing countries would face food shortages and food insecurity as a result of the virus.

HUNGER: IN YOUR FAMILY, SCHOOL, AND COMMUNITY

If you and your family are sometimes hungry, there is help. And it's okay to ask for it! Being hungry is not something anyone needs to be ashamed of or hide. If you think your family could use some help, you or a grown-up in your life can speak with a trusted adult at school, church, or elsewhere. There are food banks throughout the United States. To find one in your area, you can look here: https://www.feedingamerica.org/find-your-local -foodbank.

Do you have enough food, but you worry that your friend doesn't always have enough to eat? It's all right to share this with a grown-up in your life. You can also take action to raise money to help end hunger. Check out ideas at Feeding America: https://www.feedingamerica .org/ways-to-give/fundraise-for-feeding-america.

Preparing for the Future

We may never be able to truly understand what it was like to live during the Great Mortality. But learning about deadly diseases and pandemics of the past can help us in the twenty-first century to realize we're not the only ones who've had to face a mys-

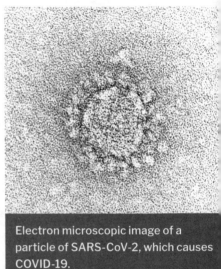

Electron microscopic image of a particle of SARS-CoV-2, which causes COVID-19.

terious and terrifying disease. And as we try to imagine life then, it also helps us realize that people in the past were afraid and sad sometimes—just as we are.

Most of all, learning about the past reminds us that diseases have always been part of human history. Diseases will always be with us—and they are sure to be part of the future.

There are several reasons for this. Despite advances in science, researchers anticipate that because of the effects of climate change and the erosion of wildlife areas and ecosystems, the chances of more viruses spreading from wildlife to humans is increasing.

Climate change, which causes droughts and more severe storms, also makes communities more vulnerable to diseases like cholera, which is waterborne, or malaria, caused by mosquitoes. Also, people who flee conflict or areas hit by rising sea levels or drought may become refugees, living in close quarters that make them more susceptible to infectious diseases like flu or COVID-19.

The challenges we face are serious. But there is hope too. We're not living in 1347, with the Great Mortality at our door. Instead, we're part of a global community of dedicated scientists, doctors, and epidemiologists with the knowledge, experience, and tools to develop vaccines, provide treatment, and find cures.

We can all be part of the effort to fight climate change, prepare for future disease outbreaks, and make life better for children and families everywhere.

It will take you and me. It will take all of us.

More for Young
Disease Detectives

GLOSSARY

ANTIBODIES Proteins that the body uses to fight off pathogens when it recognizes their antigens.

ANTIGENS Part of a pathogen that the body recognizes as foreign and fights off by producing antibodies.

ANTISEMITISM Prejudice or hostility against Jews.

BACILLUS A rod-shaped bacterium.

BACTERIA Microscopic, single-celled organisms.

BACTERIOLOGY The study of bacteria.

BACTERIUM The singular of *bacteria*.

BINOMIAL SYSTEM A system to name living things in which each name has two parts.

BLACK DEATH The plague that devastated much of the world in the mid-1300s; called the Great Mortality by the people in that era.

BLOCKED/BLOCKAGE The process by which plague bacteria block the gut of a flea, making it a more effective vector to spread the disease.

BUBOES Swollen, inflamed lymph nodes typically found in the groin, armpits, or under the ears that are symptoms of bubonic plague.

BUBONIC PLAGUE The most common form of plague, which attacks the lymph nodes.

CHRONICLE A written account or record of historical events arranged in order of time.

CHRONICLER A person who writes accounts of historical or important events.

CONTAGIOUS Contagious diseases are infectious diseases that are spread, directly or indirectly, from one person to another.

CORONAVIRUS/SARS-COV-2 The scientific name of the new strain of coronavirus that emerged in 2019 is SARS-CoV-2.

COVID-19 In people, the disease caused by the coronavirus is called Coronavirus Disease 2019, also known as COVID-19.

EPIDEMIC The outbreak of a disease that affects a large number of people within a community, population, or region.

EPIDEMIOLOGIST Someone who studies the patterns and causes of diseases and health issues in populations.

EPIDEMIOLOGY The patterns and causes of diseases and health issues in populations.

GENUS A classification category that ranks above species and below family.

GERM THEORY The currently accepted scientific premise that diseases are caused by pathogens such as bacteria and viruses.

GOLDEN HORDE A political entity called a khanate that was established in the thirteenth century in the northwestern part of the Mongol Empire.

GREAT MORTALITY The horrific outbreak of plague in the mid-1300s; also called the Black Death.

(H1N1)PDM09 VIRUS Influenza virus responsible for the 2009 "swine flu" pandemic.

INFECTIOUS DISEASES Infectious diseases are caused by pathogenic microorganisms. There are five major modes of disease transmission: airborne, waterborne, blood-borne, by direct contact, and through vectors (insects or other creatures that carry pathogens from one species to another).

INFLUENZA A viral infection that attacks the respiratory system: lungs, nose, and throat.

MEDIEVAL ERA A period in history from the fifth to the fifteenth century.

MESSENGER RNA VACCINE A vaccine developed in 2020 that teaches cells how to make a protein or part of a protein to trigger an immune response in the body.

MIASMA Bad or polluted air from rotting organic matter. The obsolete miasma theory proposed that miasma was the cause of some diseases, including cholera.

MICROBE A tiny living thing so small it can be seen only through a microscope.

MICROORGANISM Another term for a microbe.

MIDDLE AGES Another term to describe the medieval period.

MONGOL Mongols are an East Asian ethnic group native to Mongolia, a country bordered by China and

Russia. The Mongol Empire of the thirteenth and fourteenth centuries was the largest connected land empire in history.

OUTBREAK A sudden upsurge or increase in a disease.

PANDEMIC A disease outbreak that occurs globally or over a wide region.

PERSONAL PROTECTIVE EQUIPMENT (PPE) Face masks and other gear used to help protect people from transmitting or contracting some infectious diseases.

PHYSICAL DISTANCING The practice of keeping a safe space between oneself and others, especially in public, to reduce the chance of transmitting disease.

PLAGUE A severe bacterial disease that usually spreads from an animal host to humans through a vector, such as a flea.

PNEUMONIC PLAGUE A lethal form of plague that attacks the lungs and is highly contagious.

POGROM Organized riot, violence, or massacre of an ethnic group, particularly violence aimed at Jews.

PRIMARY SOURCE An artifact, document, illustration, photograph, diary, or account created during the time being studied, and which often serves as a source of direct information.

PROTISTS Single-cell organisms of the kingdom *Protista*, such as algae.

QUARANTINE A period of isolation used for people or animals who have been exposed to a disease, or are arriving from somewhere else.

SEPTICEMIC PLAGUE A deadly form of plague that infects the blood.

SPANISH FLU A nickname for the most severe pandemic in modern history, an H1N1 flu strain spread around the world in 1918, believed to have caused 50 million deaths worldwide with about 675,000 occurring in the United States.

SPECIES A group of living organisms capable of interbreeding. People are the species *Homo sapiens* and are the only members of the *Homo* genus not extinct.

TATAR Turkic people who ruled central Asia in the fourteenth century.

YERSINIA PESTIS The bacterium that causes plague, named for Dr. Alexandre Yersin.

VARIOLA VIRUS Viral infection that caused smallpox.

VIRUS A virus is one or more molecules surrounded by a protein shell. Since they have no cells of their own, viruses are not considered by scientists to be actual living organisms.

WHO The World Health Organization is an agency of the United Nations founded in 1948 to focus on international public health.

ZOONOTIC DISEASES Illnesses that are caused by germs that spread from animals to people.

TEST YOUR KNOWLEDGE
Fill in the blanks

A small insect called a rat flea often serves as a _____ for plague transmission to people.

A _____ is a large outbreak of disease that may affect many countries in the world.

Plague can now be treated early with _____.

COVID-19 is caused by a _____.

In 1854 London, Dr. John Snow tried to prove that cholera wasn't caused by bad air but by _____.

Scientists who study the patterns of disease are called

_____.

Those who lived through the most intense outbreak of plague in medieval times called it the _____.

_____ is the only infectious disease that has been eliminated successfully.

DISEASE ACTIVITIES

Pandemic Unscramble

VEORCT

NATAUIRNQE

MECDIEIP

LPEUGA

LAFE

OLPTSOIIGEDEMI

EIMNUCPON

BUCINBO

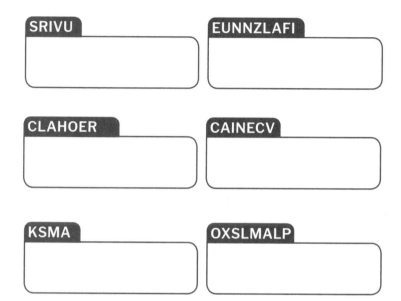

SRIVU

EUNNZLAFI

CLAHOER

CAINECV

KSMA

OXSLMALP

BE A TWENTY-FIRST-CENTURY CHRONICLER

"I miss my friends, but I like spending time with my family."

—HUDSON, AGE 7,
NEW YORK CITY,
SUMMER 2020

In this book, we read the words of chroniclers such as Gabriele de' Mussi, whose words help us understand events of nearly seven hundred years ago. What would people in the fourteenth century think about our lives today?

Pretend you're creating a chronicle that someone seven hundred years from now might read. What would you want to say about your life? What everyday details would you like to share—details that might seem normal to us but surprising to someone from another time?

To write a chronicle, you might choose to share who you are and where you live, what you like to do, and what happens each day. Or you could write about quarantining during the 2020 pandemic. Here are some ideas for things to include.

- Your name and date of birth.
- Where you were born and the names of parents, relatives, guardians, friends, or siblings.
- A description of where you live and the name of your city or town.
- Write down your favorite meal, or some of the things you like to do. Make sure you include details. For instance, if you like to read, give the title of the book, the author, and what it's about.

Meet Some Coronavirus Chroniclers

I'd like you to meet some middle schoolers at Lake Champlain Waldorf School who took on the challenge of becoming Coronavirus Chroniclers in 2020, thanks to their teacher, Rebekah Hopkinson. (And, yes, there's a connection: She's my daughter.) I hope these pieces inspire you, your family, your class, or your friends to become chroniclers too.

> It was very weird in the beginning of the lockdown when all of a sudden in-person school stopped and school went online. We didn't leave unless it was for essential purposes, when we did leave we had to wear masks.
>
> —ALEXIS GERLACK

Dear COVID-19,

When you came to America, I think we finally realized you were here when you shut down sports. As a three-sport athlete and a very athletic family, we were just getting ready for the spring season of lacrosse. You shut it down and made me realize how much I lived for sports. On the weekend we would normally find a basketball, soccer, baseball, football, or almost any other sports game and watch it. But when you came to town we were watching marble races or really old basketball games. It was fun for a little bit but then I got bored of watching the same thing over and over again.

I know things will never be the same, and you have helped me realize how much I love sports and how much I need them in my life. You have also helped me want to watch more women's sports and make sure that if we are going to watch the Portland Blazers, we need to watch the Seattle Storm too. I am thankful that you are taking a little break right now, and I know that you have changed sports forever and I might not forgive you for that. But I do want to thank you for helping me realize how much I love sports and you have made me realize that women's basketball is no different and still has all the stars. Please don't take sports away from me again.

Odile J. Elliott

I MISS . . .

I miss my school, my friends.

I can't stand thinking that

when I go back, everything will have changed.

The people who I'm close to may no longer be there.

Because schools are closed the things I love to do

are being canceled.

I miss knowing that whenever I need a hug,

I can just look over at my friends and feel better.

I miss knowing that on Monday morning,

everything will be OK.

Eden Belle

Living during the COVID-19 pandemic has been rough for everyone. It's been hard having people look at you as though you are a walking germ. It feels like the world has shrunk, for people barely recognize anyone, with half our face covered, and when you are recognized, it is a minor miracle. An upside has been that more homeless pets have been adopted, because people have been home more often. But despite some upsides, people have been heartbroken, having to say their last and first words on FaceTime. I find myself wondering what has happened to the place we all called home.

Isabella B. Gravina-Budis

EMOTION

No matter how much

Comfort.

Love.

Distraction.

I have I still feel

empty

Love.

Hate

Fear.

They are always here.

They wait.

Despair

Joy

The Deadliest Diseases Then and Now

They leave a tear
In the strongest.

Luna Van Deusen

Trying to stay positive while staying negative.

Flora Diehl-Noble

RECOMMENDATIONS FOR
FURTHER READING

Brown, Don. *Fever Year: The Killer Flu of 1918*. New York: HMH Books for Young Readers, 2019.

Hopkinson, Deborah. *The Great Trouble: A Mystery of London, the Blue Death, and a Boy Called Eel*. New York: Knopf, 2013.

Marrin, Alfred. *Very, Very, Very Dreadful: The Influenza Pandemic of 1918*. New York: Knopf, 2018.

Marshall, Linda Elovitz. Illustrated by Lisa Anchin. *The Polio Pioneer: Dr. Jonas Salk and the Polio Vaccine*. New York: Knopf, 2020.

Murphy, Jim. *An American Plague: The True and Terrifying Story of the Yellow Fever Epidemic of 1793*. New York: Clarion, 2003.

SELECTED BIBLIOGRAPHY

I researched this book by reading other books, looking at official websites such as the World Health Organization and the Centers for Disease Control and Prevention. Listed here are just a few of the books I found especially useful.

Aberth, John. *The Black Death: The Great Mortality of 1348–1350: A Brief History with Documents.* Boston: Bedford/St. Martin's, 2005.

Arnold, Catharine. *Pandemic 1918: Eyewitness Accounts from the Greatest Medical Holocaust in Modern History.* New York: St. Martin's Press, 2018.

Barry, John M. *The Great Influenza: The Story of the Deadliest Pandemic in History.* New York: Penguin, 2018.

Cantor, Norman F. *In the Wake of the Plague: The Black Death and the World It Made.* New York: Free Press, 2001.

Selected Bibliography

Herlihy, David. *The Black Death and the Transformation of the West*. Edited by Samuel K. Cohn, Jr. Cambridge, MA: Harvard University Press, 1997.

Horrox, Rosemary (editor and translator). *The Black Death*. Manchester, UK: Manchester University Press, 1994.

Iezzoni, Lynette. *Influenza 1918: The Worst Epidemic in American History*. New York: TV Books, 1999.

Johnson, Steven. *The Ghost Map: The Story of London's Most Terrifying Epidemic—and How It Changed Science, Cities, and the Modern World*. New York: Riverhead Books, 2006.

Kelly, John. *The Great Mortality: An Intimate History of the Black Death, the Most Devastating Plague of All Time*. New York: HarperCollins, 2005.

Kelly, Maria. *A History of the Black Death in Ireland*. Stroud, UK: Tempus, 2001.

McNeill, William H. *Plagues and Peoples*. New York: Anchor, 1977, 1989, 1998.

Oldstone, Michael B. A. *Viruses, Plagues, and History: Past, Present, and Future.* New York: Oxford University Press, 2010.

Ormrod, Mark, and Phillip Lindley (editors). *The Black Death in England, 1348–1500.* Donington, UK: Shan Tyas, 2003.

Orent, Wendy. *Plague: The Mysterious Past and Terrifying Future of the World's Most Dangerous Disease.* New York: Free Press, 2004.

Porter, Stephen. *Black Death: A New History of the Bubonic Plagues of London.* London: Amberley, 2018.

Ziegler, Philip. *The Black Death.* Wolfeboro Falls, NH: Alan Sutton Publishing, 1991. Originally published in the United Kingdom, 1969.

SOURCE NOTES

Source notes may seem boring—but they're actually really cool. They are a bit like the evidence that a detective collects to make a case. Source notes tell us where an author got a fact or a quotation. For instance, a source note should let us know if the quotation was from a letter, a book, a newspaper article, or an oral history.

A note to teachers, educators, librarians, and adult readers: I believe that young readers deserve nonfiction based on the latest academic research available. You will therefore find references to several scholarly articles included here in the notes, but for the sake of simplicity, I haven't included these sources in the Selected Bibliography.

The Deadliest Diseases Then and Now

Part One

"And were it not . . .": Boccaccio, in Horrox, 28.

Chapter 1
200 million: Kelly, J., 11.

Mongol ruler: ibid., 6.

"'This is the grave . . .'": Orent, 104

New research by Dr. Monica Green: Dr. Green writes about the global history of the Great Mortality and also edits articles in *Pandemic Disease in the Medieval World: Rethinking the Black Death*, ARC Medieval Press, 2015. https://library.oapen .org/bitstream/handle/20.500.12657/42786/9781942401018 .pdf?sequence=1&isAllowed=y.

"In the 1340s . . ." Jones, in communication with author, October 2020.

Definitions: CDC, https://www.cdc.gov/csels/dsepd/ss1978/lesson1 /section11.html.

Chapter 2
"We were carrying the darts . . .": de Mussi[s], in Horrox, 19.

"What seemed like mountains . . .": ibid., 17.

New Research by Hannah Barker: Barker, H. "Laying the Corpses to Rest: Grain Embargoes and the Early Transmission of the Black Death in the Black Sea, 1346–1347," *Speculum, A Journal of Medieval Studies*, 96, no. 1, January 2021. https://www.journals.uchicago.edu/doi /full/10.1086/711596.

"Some boats were bound": de Mussi[s], in Horrox, 18–19.

Black Death term: Kelly, J., 23.

Plague of Justinian: Orent, 79–80.

Third Pandemic: Plague history, *Britannica*: https://www.britannica .com/science/plague/History.

Source Notes

Chapter 3
"'It is of the form of an apple . . .'": Ziegler, 153.

streptomycin: *Britannica*, https://www.britannica.com/science/streptomycin.

Chapter 4
"They brought with them a plague . . .": da Piazza, in Aberth, 29.

Medieval shipping practices: Kelly, J., 84–85.

"They brought with them . . .": da Piazza, in Aberth, 29.

"victims violently coughed . . .": da Piazza, in Horrox, 36.

"The people of Messina . . .": ibid.

"But the illness remained . . .": ibid.

"Everyone has a responsibility . . .": de Mussi[s], in Horrox, 21.

"so that the conditions . . .": ibid., 24.

"One man there . . .": ibid., 21.

"Priests and doctors . . .": ibid., 19.

"First, out of the blue . . .": ibid., 24.

"Behold the swellings . . .": ibid.

"doctors could not know . . . ": Jones, in communication with author, October 2020.

"But what made . . .": Boccaccio, in Horrox, 27–28.

"They refrained . . .": ibid., 28–29.

"In the face . . .": ibid., 27.

Florence mortality rate: Cesana, Benedictow, Bianucci, "The Origin and Early Spread of the Black Death in Italy: First Evidence of Plague Victims from 14th-Century Liguria (Northern Italy)," *Anthropological Science*, Vol. 125 (I), 15–24, 2017, 17.

Chapter 5
"And I call the mortality great . . .": de Chauliac, in Aberth, 64.

"continuous fever . . .": ibid, 63.

"And the mortality was . . .": ibid., 64.

"Nonetheless, toward the end . . .": ibid., 66.

"Many were uncertain . . .": ibid., 64–65.

Chapter 6

"'It is seething, terrible . . .'": Gethin, in Ziegler, 153.

"'There can be no one . . .'": Porter, 57.

about seventy-five thousand: ibid., 72.

"This pestilence held . . .": Burton, in Horrox, 69.

"It first began . . .": Clynn, in Horrox, 82–83.

"Since the beginning of the world . . .": ibid., 83–84.

"And I, Brother John . . .": ibid., 84.

"Here it seems . . .": ibid., 42.

Part Two

"'The world is changed . . .'": Kelly, J., 286.

Chapter 7

"'But it was not only . . .'": Richard Bradley in Cynthia Wall's "Notes" for Daniel Defoe, *A Journal of the Plague Year* (New York: Penguin Classics, 2003), 242–43.

Chapter 8

"The fees were low . . .": Wu Lien-teh (ed.), *Manchurian Plague Prevention Service, Memorial Volume, 1912–1932* (Shanghai: National Quarantine Service, 1934), "Autobiography," 459. (Hereafter "Autobiography.")

"to keep my head above . . .": ibid., 460.

"small stocky spindles . . .": Alexandre Yersin, Pasteur Institute,

Source Notes

https://www.pasteur.fr/en/research-journal/news/alexandre-yersin-man-who-discovered-bacterium-responsible-plague.

"'I took advantage . . .'": Simond, Godley, Mouriquand, "Paul-Louis Simond and His Discovery of Plague Transmission by Rat Fleas: A Centenary," *Journal of the Royal Society of Medicine*, Vol. 91, February 1998, 101–4, 102, https://www.ncbi.nlm.nih.gov/pmc/articles/PMC1296502/.

"'By the evening . . .'": ibid.

"up to then . . .": Wu, "Autobiography," 462–63.

"the healthy marmot . . .": Wu, Inaugural Address, International Plague Conference, Mukden, China, April 4, 1911, p. 2, https://archive.org/details/b22437071/page/n1/mode/2up.

"when the marmot . . .": ibid.

"The third pandemic . . . ": https://www.who.int/csr/resources/publications/surveillance/plague.pdf.

San Francisco: https://www.pbs.org/wgbh/aso/databank/entries/dm00bu.html.

Number of deaths: *Britannica*, https://www.britannica.com/science/plague/History.

Chapter 9
Madagascar: Randremanana et al., "Epidemiological Characteristics of an Urban Plague Epidemic in Madagascar, August–November, 2017: An Outbreak Report," *The Lancet*, March 28, 2019. WHO: https://apps.who.int/iris/bitstream/handle/10665/259556/Ex-PlagueMadagascar04122017.pdf;jsessionid=1447D1CB6F7E6E685B1D47C70C53FDCB?sequence=1.

Chapter 10
Fort Riley: Iezzoni, 23.

three waves: CDC, 1918 flu pandemic, https://www.cdc.gov/flu/pandemic-resources/1918-commemoration/three-waves.htm.

The Deadliest Diseases Then and Now

2009 Swine Flu Pandemic: CDC, 2009 H1N1 Pandemic (H1N1pdm09) virus, https://www.cdc.gov/flu/pandemic-resources/2009-h1n1-pandemic .html#:~:text=From%20April%2012%2C%202009%20to,the%20 (H1N1)pdm09%20virus.

"A flu vaccine . . .": CDC, "Key Facts about Seasonal Flu Vaccine," https://www.cdc.gov/flu/prevent/keyfacts.htm.

Part Four

Chapter 11
300 million smallpox deaths: WHO, https://www.who.int/about/bugs _drugs_smoke_chapter_1_smallpox.pdf.

"Almost two centuries . . .": CDC, "History of Smallpox," https:// www.cdc.gov/smallpox/history/history.html#:~:text=Almost%20 two%20centuries%20after%20Jenner,achievement%20in%20 international%20public%20health.

"'Now when I meet . . .'": Meissner, H. Cody, "What Is Ali Maalin's Claim to Fame?" *AAP News (Official Newsmagazine of the American Academy of Pediatrics)*, Vol. 35, Number 3, March 2014. https://www .aappublications.org/content/35/3/7.1.

HIV: WHO. https://www.who.int/gho/hiv/en/.

Part Five

Chapter 12
Mattia: Donadio, Rachel, "I can't stop thinking about Patient One," *Atlantic*, April 16, 2020, https://www.theatlantic.com/international /archive/2020/04/italy-patient-one-family-coronavirus-covid19/610039/.

WHO declared: https://www.who.int/dg/speeches/detail/who-director -general-s-opening-remarks-at-the-media-briefing-on-covid -19---11-march-2020.

United Nations World Food Program estimated: https://www.nytimes .com/2020/09/11/world/covid-19-coronavirus.html#link-393ad215.

PHOTOGRAPH AND ILLUSTRATION CREDITS

Photos ©: **Adobe Stock:** cover (Gonzalo), cover (vespera); **Alamy Images:** 149 (Science History Images); **Center for Disease Control and Prevention:** 18, 41 top, 41 bottom, 42, 134-135 (Paul Howell/Janice Haney Carr), 143 (World Health Organization), 145, 148 (James Goodson, MPH), 154-155, 160 (National Center for Immunization and Respiratory Diseases (NCIRD), Division of Viral Diseases), 164 (Cynthia S. Goldsmith/Azaibi Tamin), 166 (Amy Schuh, PhD, MPH); **Dreamstime:** 15 (Vladimir Krotov); **Getty Images:** cover (Romaoslo), 109 (Hulton Archive); **Library of Congress:** 91, 118; **National Archives:** 119; **National Museum of Health and Medicine:** 122; **New Zealand Ministry of Health:** 151; **Roger**

INDEX

Page numbers in *italics* refer to illustrations.

ACKNOWLEDGMENTS

I've long been fascinated by the history of medicine and science. And several years ago, when Scholastic editor Lisa Sandell and I discussed the Deadliest series, writing about diseases and the Great Mortality was at the top of my list. However, neither editor Lisa nor I ever imagined that we—and the rest of the world—would be living through a deadly pandemic as the book was being written.

I am enormously fortunate to be able to work with the incomparable Lisa Sandell once again. Her wisdom, patience, and guidance never falters. In addition, I am grateful to my agent Steven Malk and his team, as well as the entire Scholastic team, including Jordana Kulak, Rachel Feld, Julia Eisler, Olivia Valcarce, Keirsten Geise, Jael Fogle, Lori Benton, Ellie Berger, Erin

Berger, David Levithan, Elizabeth Parisi, John Pels, Becky Terhune, Cian O'Day, Emily Teresa, Matthew Poulter, Danielle Yadao, Alan Smagler, Elizabeth Whiting, Jarad Waxman, Dan Moser, Jackie Rubin, and the whole sales team. Special thanks too, to the wonderful Lizette Serrano, Emily Heddleson, Robin Hoffman, Laura Beets, and the entire Book Fairs team, including the inspiring Mr. John Schu. Thank you! It is an honor and privilege to work with you all.

Any errors or mistakes in the manuscript are my own. There would be many more, however, were it not for the incredibly important contribution of Dr. Lori Jones, medical historian at the University of Ottawa and Carleton University in Ottawa, Canada. Not only did she correct errors and improve the manuscript considerably, she shared cutting-edge research. Her main area of expertise is medical writing about the plague. She is known for her work on detecting images from the past that have been labeled incorrectly as being from the Great Mortality. Dr. Jones works with historians